EVE

Valentine

Heartwarming Stories of Love

EVERYTHING

Valentine

Heartwarming Stories of Love

Tonya Lambert

BLUE
BIKE
BOOKS

© 2013 by Blue Bike Books Ltd.
First printed in 2013 10 9 8 7 6 5 4 3 2 1
Printed in Canada

The Publisher: Blue Bike Books

Website: www.bluebikebooks.com

Library and Archives Canada Cataloguing in Publication

Lambert, Tonya, author
     Everything Valentine: heartwarming stories of love / Tonya Lambert.

ISBN 978-1-926700-44-1 (pbk.)

     1. Valentine's Day—Miscellanea. I. Title.

GT4925.L36 2013   394.2618   C2013-907556-9

Project Director: Nicholle Carrière
Project Editor: Sheila Quinlan
Front and Back Cover Images: Background with floating hearts border © sunnyfrog / iStock; heart made of roses © Joe Biafore / iStock; diamond heart, lips heart and balloon heart © Denys Fonchykov / Photos.com; heart made of candies © Tomasz Wyszoamirski / Photos.com; shiny glossy red heart © Chris Gorgio / Photos.com
Illustrations: All illustrations are sourced from Photos.com, with the exception of the following: Roger Garcia 113, 176, 216; Library of Congress 62, 83; Peter Tyler 117. © *Photos.com:* Alina Utter 189; Anastasiya Zalevska 201; catrinka81 137; d_rich 167; dapoomll 181; Dynamic Graphics 19, 40, 78, 102, 106, 122, 126, 147, 154, 172, 185, 193, 198; Evrensel Baris Berkant 44; Jupiterimages 11, 22, 25, 66, 70, 98, 132, 143, 151, 158, 205, 210, 220; lhfgraphics 138; loliputa 52; Marina Datsenko 14; Naddiya 93; Pavel Kvach 47; Photos.com 31, 58, 86; ryan burke 110; Steven Wynn 35; Vanda Grigorovic 162; Wojciech Plonka 91.

Produced with the assistance of the Government of Alberta, Alberta Media Fund.

We acknowledge the financial support of the Government of Canada through the Canada Book Fund (CBF) for our publishing activities.

Canadian   Patrimoine
Heritage   canadien

PC: 24

DEDICATION
For my Grandma
Evaline Quinnell Campbell (1909–2005)
Dearly loved; greatly missed.

CONTENTS

LONELY HEARTS AND LUSTFUL TEMPTATIONS: ANTI-VALENTINE'S SENTIMENTS

ACKNOWLEDGMENTS

I would like to thank my daughters, Becky, Mary and Amy, for all their support, encouragement and ideas.

A big thanks goes to my publisher, Nicholle Carrière, for her advice, guidance and support.

Finally, thank you to Andrea and Gordon.

INTRODUCTION

Valentine's Day—either you love it or you hate it. No other holiday in the Western world creates such extreme yet opposite feelings. Just hearing the name of this holiday can arouse strong emotions in people.

Valentine's Day is a holiday meant for people in love. It is a day for couples. If you happen to be part of a couple then there is a good chance you love Valentine's Day. For someone in love, Valentine's Day is a day when that love is highlighted and paraded about for all to see. It is a day to give and receive gifts; a day to go out and do fun, romantic things with your significant other or stay in and enjoy some intimate time together. It is a day when you are reminded that you are loved, cared for, supported and appreciated.

If you are not part of a couple, Valentine's Day is just the opposite. No other day of the year (except perhaps the date of a particularly painful break-up) can make the single person feel more alone, more unloved. Everywhere a person looks at this time of year, they see reminders of everything they do not have in their life. Sure, family and friends can be supportive, but it is not the same thing, and the cupids, hearts and smiling couples are painful indicators of that fact.

In a world where divorce rates are higher than ever and people are marrying (if they marry at all) at a later age, more and more people are finding themselves single on Valentine's Day. This rise in singles has led to the development of two new celebrations on February 14: Single Awareness Day (or Quirkyalone Day) and Anti-Valentine's Day. The former celebrates the single life, while the latter just allows people to vent their frustration at the holiday, whether that frustration is directed at happy couples or at the commercialism of the day.

Some people dislike Valentine's Day not because they object to the idea behind the day but because they believe that the marketing push is so great that it takes away from what the day is supposed to express—love for one another. Commercials dictate what those expressions of love are supposed to look like and create expectations in people that often lead to disappointments. Ever since Valentine's cards were first sold in stores in the early 19th century, critics have warned that purchasing prepackaged sentiments takes away from the authenticity of the feelings expressed.

With such strong emotions brewing all around, it should come as no surprise that Valentine's Day leads to a spike in all types of occurrences—engagements and weddings, but also break-ups, divorces and suicides. Some countries (mainly Islamic ones) have banned the celebration of Valentine's Day altogether, seeing it as more of a day of lust than of love. Individual schools are also curtailing festivities for a variety of reasons, but most seem to center on the notion of not having students feeling left out.

In still other parts of the world, like Latin America, or even in individual households, Valentine's Day has taken on a more inclusive nature. It has become a day to celebrate all types of love, not just the romantic love that exists between members of a couple. Friendships are celebrated. Love between a parent and child is honored. Even the collegial relationship that exists between co-workers is sometimes recognized with a small gift, such as a card or a chocolate.

Whether you love Valentine's Day or hate it, it has been a part of the culture of the English- and French-speaking worlds for over 700 years, and it is expanding to include much of the rest of the world. Valentine's Day is not going away anytime soon. Hopefully, this book is both entertaining and informative for proponents and critics of Valentine's Day alike, as well as the merely curious.

SAINTS AND LOVERS: VALENTINE'S DAY ORIGINS

Creating a Day for Lovers

For this was on seynt Valentynes Day, Whan every foul cometh ther to choose his mate.

–Geoffrey Chaucer, "Parliament of Fowls" (1382)

The first person to write about a connection between the feast day of St. Valentine and love was the English poet Geoffrey Chaucer (d. 1400). Chaucer is familiar to anyone who studied parts of his *Canterbury Tales* in school. But Chaucer was not just a poet; he was also a diplomat and bureaucrat.

In 1382, Chaucer wrote the poem that we know today as the "Parliament of Fowls." This poem is believed to be the first linking of St. Valentine's Day with romantic love. The poem was written to celebrate the first anniversary of the engagement of the English king Richard II and his first wife, Anne of Bohemia. Their marriage treaty had been signed on May 2, 1381.

Chaucer went on to refer to St. Valentine's Day as a time for love in at least two other poems. The day was the setting for his "Complaint of Mars"; and in the prologue to the "Legend of Good Women," which Chaucer wrote for Queen Anne, he writes of birds choosing their mates on St. Valentine's Day just as he did in the "Parliament of Fowls" (see quote on previous page). A third poem, "Complaynt d'Amours," which some scholars ascribe to Chaucer, has the poet avow his love for his lady on St. Valentine's Day and always, just as birds choose their mates then.

Pick a Valentine, Any Valentine

The historian Henry Ansgar Kelly has convincingly argued that the St. Valentine's Day referred to by Chaucer was that of St. Valentine of Genoa, on May 3. Kelly bases his argument on political events, astronomy and seasonal references, such as the mating of birds. He argues that Chaucer chose St. Valentine of Genoa over the more well-known St. Valentine of Terni in order to honor his monarch's betrothal. Chaucer is known to have traveled to Genoa a few years earlier on a diplomatic mission and was likely introduced to this St. Valentine while there.

Kelly shows that within a generation, the timing of the celebration had switched to February 14, the feast of the more widely known St. Valentine, the martyred bishop of Terni. The poets, however, continued to refer to the mating of birds as occurring on St. Valentine's Day, just as Chaucer had in his original Valentine's Day poems.

DID YOU KNOW?

The poem "The Book of Cupid," sometimes attributed to Sir John Clanvowe (d. 1391), places St. Valentine's Day in March.

St. Valentine of Genoa

St. Valentine of Genoa is credited with several miracles. A man was saved from choking on a bone by praying to the saint in the Church of St. Syrus. A woman whose face had become swollen and discolored was returned to normal after praying to the saint. A sick girl from Asti was brought to the church in Genoa by her parents. Too ill to walk, the girl saw an apparition of the saint approach her, and she was able to walk again. During the medieval period, the people of Genoa actively celebrated the feast day of their St. Valentine on May 2 or 3.

St. Valentine of Terni and St. Valentine of Rome

Nothing is actually known about the life of the man who has lent his name to an almost global celebration of love. The first mention of a martyr named Valentine killed at Terni, a city in Umbria, is in a fifth-century collection of tales about early martyrs. By the eighth century, a legend had arisen surrounding the life of this man, of which probably very little, if any, is true. Nonetheless, this is how the story goes.

Valentine was the bishop of Terni. For reasons that are unclear, he was invited to Rome to try to cure the son of the pagan orator Crato. Valentine moved into the family's villa, and when he was not attending to the son's health, he debated philosophy and religion with the father. Valentine's trip to Rome was a success: he cured the son, and the entire family was baptized into the Christian faith. Spurred on by his accomplishments, Valentine stayed on in Rome, preaching the new religion and converting more people. Eventually, his efforts came to the attention of the Roman prefect Placidius, who did not appreciate Valentine's efforts to turn the citizens of Rome away from the official state religion. On Placidius' orders, Valentine was captured and beaten to death, then buried along the Flaminian Way going through his home city of Terni.

Supposedly another man named Valentine was martyred at Rome around this time, that is, in the third century. As with St. Valentine of Terni, nothing is known for sure about this man known as St. Valentine of Rome. The stories surrounding these two men have become intertwined and have been added to over time, to the point where the Catholic Church removed the feast day of St. Valentine from the official church calendar in 1969.

The earliest story of St. Valentine of Rome is from the fifth century. This Valentine was a Roman priest who, because of his religion, was placed under house arrest in the villa of another Roman prefect, this one named Calpurnius. St. Valentine of Rome healed the child of the prefect, in this case his blind daughter, as well as managing to convert the entire household to Christianity. And like his namesake from Terni, he was beaten to death and buried along the Flaminian Way. Both men are said to have met their deaths on February 14—it's easy to see how the lives of the two men came to be conflated. Or maybe there was only one martyr named Valentine in third-century Rome, who somehow over time morphed into two separate men.

These early legends surrounding the saint or saints named Valentine were elaborated throughout the following centuries. At some point, St. Valentine became a defender of marriage, and it was reported that when he was imprisoned by the emperor, he secretly married soldiers and their sweethearts even though it was illegal for soldiers to marry. It was this crime that got him executed. The other popular tale of St. Valentine is that he became good friends with the blind girl whose sight he was able to restore. After his imprisonment and shortly before his execution, he was able to get a letter out to this girl that he signed, "From your Valentine." Both stories are nice, but almost definitely nothing but stories and almost certainly arose after the feast day of the saint became associated with love and courtship.

Nonetheless, a martyr named Valentine was accorded sainthood by Pope Gelasius I in 496 and given the feast day of February 14. St. Valentine has come to be the patron saint of not only lovers but also of beekeepers, epileptics and plague sufferers.

I claim there ain't
Another Saint
As great as Valentine.

–Ogden Nash (1902–1971)

More St. Valentines!
If you are not already confused enough, here is a list of several more saints named Valentine:

- In Bavaria, the feast day St. Valentine, bishop of Passau, is on January 7.

- A St. Valentine, along with his companions St. Marius, St. Martha and others, was honored on January 19 at Rome.

- The church of St. Charles at Turin is supposed to be the final resting place of another martyred St. Valentine. His feast is celebrated on March 2.

- ♥ In Syria, a St. Valentine and nine others had their feast day on March 20.

- ♥ An early martyrology mentions April 29 as the feast day of St. Valentine and St. Marcian of Perugia.

- ♥ In 1260, 49 Dominican friars, including a Blessed Valentine, were martyred by the Tartars at Sandomierz, Poland. Their feast is held on June 2.

- ♥ In Dijon, France, July 4 was the feast day of St. Valentine, priest of Lassois.

- ♥ St. Valentine, priest of Viterbo, had his feast day on November 3.

- ♥ In Ravenna, Italy, three saints named Valentine had feast days on November 11, November 13 and December 16.

Where Are You, Valentine?

Over the years, a number of churches, monasteries and cathedrals have claimed to house the body of St. Valentine. Here is just a small list of the claimants.

💜 The Church of San Sebastiano at Rome claims to house the head of the Roman St. Valentine.

💜 The Spanish monastery at Baga claims that the body of St. Valentine of Terni lies within its walls, while his head is in Toro.

💜 In the Church of St. Praxedes in Rome is a glass reliquary allegedly containing the bones of St. Valentine and St. Zeno.

💜 The German town of Kiedrich has a Church of St. Valentine where the head of St. Valentine of Terni is said to rest.

💜 In the 10th century, Abbot Guarinus of Cuxa is said to have brought the bones of St. Valentine to his monastery in the south of France.

💜 Emma of Normandy, wife first to King Ethelred II (d. 1016) and then to King Cnut (d. 1035) of England, donated the head of a St. Valentine as a relic to the abbey at Winchester, where the monks celebrated his feast day on February 14. The head of St. Valentine at Winchester was originally housed in the monastery at Jumièges in Normandy. Supposedly a monk returning from a trip to Terni had brought the head to the monastery. The Norman monks reportedly successfully used this relic to fend off two fires, a drought, a plague of mouse-like creatures, two great sicknesses and four cases of blindness or insanity.

💜 In the French community of St-Paulien, a church claimed to house the bones of St. Valentine and St. Albinus. Their reliquary was destroyed during the Revolution.

💜 A church at Annecy in France also claimed to house the relics of St. Valentine.

💜 In 1835, Father John Sprett (1797–1871), head of the Carmelite order in Ireland, received a gift from Pope Gregory XVI—the bones believed to be those of St. Valentine. The black and gold casket that holds the bones is put on display each Valentine's Day in Dublin's Whitefriar Street Church.

💜 Holy Trinity Church in Beresteczko, Ukraine, is also said to house the relics of St. Valentine. The Chapel of St. Valentine in this church is said to have been the scene of many miraculous healings of crippled people over the years.

💜 Glasgow, Scotland, claims to be the resting place for the remains of St. Valentine. The Church of the Blessed St. John Dun Scotus is said to hold the remains.

💜 The Church of St. Valentine in Terni probably has the best claim to house the bones of the first St. Valentine.

Richard and Anne: the Original Valentine's Day Love Story

The royal couple for whose union Chaucer is thought to have created a day of love were the boy-king Richard II and his young bride Anne of Bohemia. Like all royal marriages of the time, the couple's match had been arranged to secure a political alliance—in this case between England and the Holy Roman Empire. Anne's late father was Emperor Charles IV, and a brother would later become Emperor Sigismund. The alliance, which was approved by Pope Urban VI, strengthened the English allegiance for the Roman pope against the French allegiance for the Avignon pope, Clement VII.

When the couple married in 1382, Richard was only 15 and Anne 16. Despite the general unpopularity of the alliance among the people of England, the marriage itself seems to have flourished. The two royals were rarely apart, having grown quite fond of one another. The marriage was not blessed with any children, yet Richard never considered setting Anne aside in order to remarry and produce an heir. Indeed, Richard was remarkably faithful to his wife and left no known illegitimate offspring either.

Richard became king of England at the tender age of 10 and spent the rest of his life trying to compete with the larger-than-life memory of his father, the Black Prince. His pride, insecurity and bad temper resulted in regular quarrels with others, and Anne often had to intercede to secure the peace.

Then, in 1394, the bubonic plague struck England once again. Anne fell ill at the Palace of Sheen and died. Richard was devastated. For a year, he refused to set foot in any room that Anne had once entered. Finally, he ordered that the Palace at Sheen be torn down altogether, even though he had earlier been responsible for a great deal of its construction because it had been the favorite residence of the couple. Richard had a grave monument made for himself and Anne in the newly built Westminster Abbey. Richard and Anne were carved in stone lying side by side, holding hands for all eternity.

In 1399, Richard was forced to abdicate the throne in favor of his cousin, Henry Bolingbroke (later Henry IV). When the former king died six months later on or about Valentine's Day 1400, Henry ignored his request to be buried next to Anne and had him buried in a Dominican friary at King's Langley. When Henry's son succeeded him to the throne, he had Richard's body exhumed and reburied in Westminster Abbey next to the woman he had loved so much.

Valentine's First Poets: Chaucer, Grandson and Gower

Chaucer was friends with two other poets whose surviving works include references to the new festival of love known as St. Valentine's Day. These poets are Othon de Grandson (d. 1397) and John Gower (d. 1408).

Othon de Grandson was a knight and troubadour from Savoy who wrote several poems about the celebration of love on St. Valentine's Day. Indeed, nearly a third of his poems are devoted to the subject, including "St. Valentine's Dream," "St. Valentine's Day" I and II and "St. Valentine's Wish."

In one of Grandson's poems, the narrator sees others happily choosing their loves on St. Valentine's Day while he mourns the death of his love. St. Valentine and the God of Love urge him to choose a new love, which he does.

In another of his Valentine's poems, Grandson has an old man speak of pursuing his heart's desire and being rebuffed. But then on St. Valentine's Day, after he has given up the chase, his love (metaphorically referred to as a falcon) comes to him. Sadly, she eventually proves untrue and leaves him for another.

Little is known about the life of John Gower. He appears to have been a person of some standing because he was an acquaintance of Richard II. He was also a close friend of Geoffrey Chaucer, and quite possibly a lawyer because Chaucer gave him power of attorney to look after his affairs in England when Chaucer traveled to Genoa.

Gower mentions St. Valentine's Day in two poems, his 34th and 35th ballads. In the one poem, John Gower calls his lady love "my beautiful bird" and says he has chosen her in the same manner that the birds choose their mates on St. Valentine's Day. In the other poem, Gower remarks that the birds that have found a mate on Valentine's Day have fared better than he. These two poems were written in French.

Both Gower and Grandson follow Chaucer in mentioning St. Valentine's Day as the time when birds choose their mates. It is likely that they associated this day of love with May 3, as did Chaucer.

Valentine's Day in 15th-century England

That Valentine's Day was a new holiday likely originating in Chaucer's time, if not created by that poet himself, can be seen in the confusion that surrounded the celebration in early 15th-century England. St. Valentine was clearly not a well-known saint at the time; the timing of the feast, not to mention the gender of the saint, were uncertain to many English citizens.

Loving with Lydgate

John Lydgate (c. 1370–1451) was a monk in the Benedictine monastery at Bury St. Edmonds in Suffolk. A skilled poet, Lydgate left us three poems in which he mentions the new custom of choosing Valentines. Lydgate's poems show the somewhat confused notion of the exact timing of St. Valentine's Day that seems to have been common in the early years of the celebration. For example, in his poem "A Calendar," Lydgate chooses three different Valentines throughout the year. In February, for Valentine's Day, his choice falls on the virgin Julian; in August, for the Feast of the Assumption, he not surprisingly picks Mary; and finally in November, on All Hallows, he decides to include all the saints.

This preference for choosing religious figures as his Valentines is also found in Lydgate's poem "A Valentine to Her that Excelleth All." Written in 1440, this poem was dedicated to Queen Katherine, wife of Henry V, but was written in honor of the Virgin Mary:

> *Seynte Valentine, of custome yeere by yeere*
> *Men have an usaunce in this regioun*
> *To loke and serche Cupides Kalendere,*
> *And chose theyre choyse, by grete affeccioun;*
> *Such as ben prike with Cupides mocioun,*
> *Takyng theyre choyse as theyr sort doth falle:*
> *But I love oon which excellith alle.*

The third poem in which Lydgate discusses St. Valentine's Day is "The Flower of Courtesy." In this lengthy poem, the narrator laments that the woman he loves does not love him in return but vows to continue to love her faithfully nonetheless.

Norwich's Miss St. Valentine
The earliest non-literary reference to St. Valentine's Day in England is found in a 1415 decree from the city of Norwich. In it, St. Valentine is referred to as a woman. The decree mentions the quarrels and discord that have recently divided the city's inhabitants and declares that on St. Valentine's Day, a day of love when birds choose their mates, the people of Norwich should, rich and poor, join together in peace and harmony.

Her Right Well-beloved Valentine
The earliest surviving Valentine's Day love letters in the English language were written by Margery Brews, a gentlewoman from Norfolk, to her cousin and suitor, John Paston, in February 1477. The couple desired to marry, but Margery's father refused to provide Margery with the size of dowry that John was

demanding. Margery hoped that love would win out in the end…and it did. The couple married and had a son, William.

John was older than Margery; he was in his early thirties while she was in her late teens. John had been searching for an ideal wife for some time—that is, a woman who was reasonably attractive and from a good family with a lot of money. When he met Margery, he must have fallen in love because he married her despite her lack of money.

In her two Valentine's letters to John, Margery professes her undying love for him and the tremendous agony she feels while the matter of their betrothal is unresolved. She is sorry that she cannot get her father to provide her with a larger dowry but hopes he will be satisfied nonetheless. Her first letter is as follows:

> *Unto my right well-beloved Valentine, John Paston, squire, be this bill delivered, etc.*
>
> *Right reverent and worshipful, and my right well-beloved Valentine, I recommend myself to you, full heartily desiring to hear of your welfare, which I beseech Almighty God long for to preserve unto His pleasure, and your heart's desire. And if it please you to hear of my welfare, I am not in good health of body, nor of heart, nor shall be till I hear from you; for there knows no creature what pain that I endure, and for to be dead, I dare it not discover. And my lady my mother has labored the matter to my father full diligently, but she can no more get than you know of, for the which God knows I am full sorry. But if that you love me, as I trust verily that you do, you will not leave me therefore; for if that you had not half the livelihood that you have, for to do the greatest labor that any woman alive might, I would not forsake you. And if you command me to keep me true*

*wherever I go, I know I will do all my might you to
love and never no more. And if my friends say, that
I do amiss, they shall not me let so for to do, my heart
bids me evermore to love you truly over all earthly
things, and if they be never so great, I trust it shall be
better in time coming. No more to you at this time,
but the Holy Trinity have you in keeping. And
I beseech you that this bill be seen of no earthly creature save only yourself. And this letter was written at
Topcroft, with full heavy heart, etc.*

By your own,

Margery Brews

John wrote Margery a reply indicating that he intended to come
to the Brews' home at Topcroft to reach some sort of resolution
with Margery's father regarding her dowry and their possible
bethrothal. Margery wrote to him in return:

*To my right well-beloved cousin, John Paston, squire,
be this letter delivered, etc.*

*Right worshipful and well-beloved Valentine, in my
most humble way, I recommend me unto you, etc. And
heartily I thank you for the letter which that you sent
me by John Bekarton, whereby I understand and
know, that you be purposed to come to Topcroft in
short time, and without any errand or matter, but
only to have a conclusion of the matter between my
father and you; I would be most glad of any creature
alive, so that the matter might grow to effect. And
there as you say, and you come and find the matter no
more towards you than you did before time, you would
no more put my father and my lady my mother to no
cost nor business, for that cause, a good while after,*

which causes my heart to be full heavy; and if that you come, and the matter take to some effect, then should I be much more sorry and full of heaviness.

And as for myself, I have done and understood in the matter that I can or may, as God knows, and I let you plainly understand, that my father will no more money part with all in that behalf, but £100 and 1 mark which is right far from the accomplishment of your desire.

Wherefore, if that you could be content with that good, and my poor person, I would be the merriest maiden on earth; and if you think not yourself so satisfied, or that you have much more good, as I have understood by you before; good, true, and loving Valentine, that you take no such labor upon you, as to come more for that matter, but let it pass, and never more be spoken of, as I may be your true lover and companion during my life.

No more unto you at this time, but, Almighty Jesus preserve you, both body and soul, etc.

By your Valentine,

Margery Brews

DID YOU KNOW?

Another early mention of a Valentine comes from a will from 1535 in which the writer left his money "to my valentyn Agnes Illyon."

The Court of Love: Valentine's Day in 15th-century France

Two medieval charters proclaim the annual festival of the Court of Love (*Cour Amoureuese*) on February 14 in 1401. Membership in the court was the elite of French society (including the king)—over 600 members in all. They were divided into 17 different ranks, including the Prince of Love and others from Grand Conservateurs to Gardeners. At one point, the Prince of the Court of Love was Pierre de Hauteville, Lord of Ars and Cupbearer to the King. He was the leader of a group of poets known as the "Chapel vert."

The Charter of the Court of Love stated that a mass would be sung in memory of St. Valentine every year on February 14 at the Church of St. Catherine du Val des Ecoliers in Paris. Members of the court would meet on the first Sunday of every month to feast in honor of love. An extra-special feast was to be held annually on the evening of February 14. Additional festivities were to be held on each of the five feast days honoring the Virgin Mary, as well as on a day in May.

It is appropriate that a poet such as Pierre de Hauteville should have been the Prince of the Court of Love, as the composition of love poems played a central role in the group. Men were expected to write a love poem to present at the feast in February. The women would judge the poems and choose a winner.

Scholars are divided as to whether these documents refer to a real event or whether the Court of Love is simply a literary device. However, in my opinion, the evidence points to the Court of Love being an actual event. In her two Valentine's Day poems, Christine de Pisan (b. 1364) has men and women choosing their partners on St. Valentine's Day and then renewing their pledges of love at festivities in May, just as described in the charters. She wrote that couples were supposed to awake early on February 14 and exchange green chaplets to symbolize their love for each other—appropriate, as "Chapel vert" was the name of the group of poets of which de Hauteville, Prince of the Court of Love, was the leader. Furthermore, de Pisan wrote "Le Dit de la Rose" on St. Valentine's Day in 1402 after attending King Charles VI's Court of Love, she says. She dedicated this poem to Louis I, Duke of Orleans. Louis' son Charles, also later Duke of Orleans (1394–1465), wrote more than a dozen Valentine's Day poems. In his earliest such poem, "La retinue d'Amours," he describes something very much like the new Court of Love. There is feasting and merrymaking in a castle where he is given membership in a group that centers on love.

DID YOU KNOW?

February, the month in which the western celebration of love (and some say lust) falls, derives its name from the Latin word meaning "to purify."

Poets of the Court of Love

An annual poetry competition was held on Valentine's Day as part of the new Court of Love. A number of French Valentine's Day poems survive from the 15th century. They were all likely inspired by this new holiday and custom, even if not all of them were written specifically for the competition itself.

The earliest French Valentine's poem was written in England by Charles, Duke of Orleans. Orleans was captured after the great English victory at the Battle of Agincourt in 1415 and taken to England, where he was held prisoner (in luxurious accommodations) for the next 24 years. During that time he wrote many poems, including several Valentine's Day love poems. The first such poem composed during his captivity was written to his wife Isabella de Valois, whom he calls "my very gentle Valentine." It is stored in the British Library.

In "Le beau soleil le jour saint Valentin," Orleans talks of others choosing their partners on St. Valentine's Day but does not participate himself because his love has died. In a Valentine's poem entitled "Je suis desja d'amour tanné" written later on in his life, Orleans writes that he has chosen as his new love a woman who is too young for him and finds he cannot keep up with her.

In a mid-15th century verse written for the occasion, Guillaume de Monceau, Lord of Thignonville, refers to the keeping of St. Valentine's Day as a new custom. He says he will offer his heart to the woman of his choice on St. Valentine's Day, but if she spurns it, he will give it to another.

Several Valentine poems written by René d'Anjou (1409–1480), King of Sicily, survive from the mid-15th century. A recurring theme in these poems is that the narrator is too old to participate in the festivities. In René d'Anjou's "A ce jour," St. Valentine's Day falls on Ash Wednesday, causing confusion. It is resolved by observing religious devotions in the morning and choosing part-ners in the evening.

DID YOU  KNOW?

In the medieval period, the Catholic Church taught that love was the force that set everything in the world into motion. From this teaching we get the saying, "Love makes the world go 'round."

The Lupercalia and St. Valentine's Day

Antiquarians of the 17th century first suggested a connection between the pagan festival of the Lupercalia and the Christian holiday of St. Valentine's Day. There is no evidence that the two celebrations are in any way connected; the only similarities seem to be the occurrence of both festivals in mid-February and their respective connections with fertility and love.

The Lupercalia was one of the oldest festivals of ancient Rome. Held on February 15, the celebration was connected to Rome's legendary foundation by Romulus and Remus, the twin brothers who were suckled by a she-wolf. The day began in a cave believed to be the place where the babies lived with the wolf. Rituals were performed there by priests known as *luperci*. These rituals included the sacrifice of two goats and a dog, the blood of which (along with some milk) was used to anoint two specially chosen patrician youths. The youths then joined the luperci in a feast.

After the feast, the goats were skinned and the skins were cut up. The larger parts were used as clothing by the two youths while the smaller strips served as lashes for the next portion of the festivities. The strips of goat skin were known as *februae*, a term associated with purification. The two young men ran through the streets of Rome carrying their februae and lashing all the women they saw. The women did little to avoid these lashings, which were believed to purify the women they touched, thereby ensuring their fertility. According to Roman legend, the Sabine women kidnapped by the first male inhabitants of the city were barren until they had been hit with the februae.

Many Romans continued to celebrate the Lupercalia even after Christianity was declared the official religion of the empire in 380. It was not until 496 that Pope Gelasius I finally banned the celebration of the Lupercalia.

DID YOU KNOW?

In Shakespeare's *Julius Caesar*, Mark Antony runs in the Lupercalia. Caesar asks him to touch Caesar's wife, Calpurnia, so she will no longer be barren.

A HOLIDAY FOR EVERYONE: EARLY VALENTINE'S DAY CUSTOMS

A Tudor Valentine

King Henry VIII of England made Valentine's Day an official holiday in 1537, but it had been celebrated by the gentry and nobility for nearly 150 years already. It was popular at the Tudor court, especially with Henry's eldest daughter, Princess Mary.

In 1522, six-year-old Princess Mary Tudor chose the Hapsburg emperor Charles V to be her Valentine. This choice had not been left to chance but was part of the negotiations between England and Spain to form a marriage alliance between the two countries. The princess wore a gold brooch with "Charles" spelled out in jewels.

Mary's brooch was an expensive example of the "love-bagges" worn by women in England on Valentine's Day. These badges might be just a simple piece of paper with the name of the woman's Valentine written on it, but they were always worn next to the heart. Over a century later, in 1662, English civil servant Samuel Pepys (1633–1703) mentions in his diary a Mrs. T. wearing his name pinned to her breast.

In 1525, nine-year-old Mary drew the name of elderly, gout-ridden Ralph Egerton to be her Valentine. The two engaged in the customary mock romance, exchanging love letters in which Mary referred to Egerton as her "husband adoptif" and signed herself "your wyfe." At one point, Mary jokingly scolded Egerton, saying, "ye take greater care of your goute…than ye do of your wyfe."

In 1538, 22-year-old Mary drew George Mountejoy, one of her yeomen, as her Valentine and gave him 40 shillings as a gift. When Princess Mary Tudor was drawn by Sir Anthony Browne to be his Valentine in 1543, she gave him a gold-enameled brooch inset with a black agate and three small rubies. On the agate was depicted the story of Abraham from the Bible.

The Luck of the Draw

It is not known when the custom of drawing names for Valentines first began, but it was likely in the early 16th century. By 1641, it was so popular that one Edinburgh man jokingly suggested that the method be used to pick the new Lord Chancellor. The custom was quite common in 17th-century England and Scotland and continued to be widely practiced in the 18th and 19th centuries. The custom varied somewhat by region and over time.

England

Drawing lots for Valentines was a custom found in the northern part of England as well as in the London area. In the western counties, the custom of the first person one saw on Valentine's Day being one's Valentine was more popular. However, both practices could be found throughout the country as people and ideas traveled from place to place.

One of the earliest mentions of drawing names for Valentines mocked the custom. Michael Drayton (1563–1631), in his ode "To His Valentine," believed that people who drew lots for such an important matter were foolish. Drayton's sentiments were repeated in a 1645 letter from Dudley, Lord North, to his brother:

> *A lady of wit and quality whom you well know, would never put herself to the chance of a Valentine, saying that she would never couple herself but by choice. The custom and charge of Valentines is not ill left, with many other such costly and idle customs, which by a tacit general consent we lay down as obsolete.*

The Puritans in England had mixed feelings about the custom of drawing lots for Valentines. They strongly believed in pre-ordination and that everything should be done according to God's will. The idea of drawing lots was contentious because it seemed to leave things to chance. But some Puritans argued that no chance was involved because the drawing of lots was ordained by God, who knew the outcome. Others argued that it went against God's will. Ralph Levett (b. 1600) was a Puritan minister and protégé of the older minister John Cotton (1585–1652). Levett was hired to serve as clergyman to the Wray family at Ashby-cum-Fenby in Lincolnshire. While there, he faced numerous situations in which he was unsure how to act. On these occasions, he would write to his mentor for advice. One such situation involved the drawing of lots for Valentines. Two young ladies of the household approached the minister and asked him to participate. He wrote to Cotton, who confirmed his suspicion that drawing lots was wrong because it was "a takeinge of Gods name in vaine."

During the Interregnum in England (1649–1660), the Puritan government of Oliver Cromwell forbade the practice of drawing lots for Valentines. It is unlikely that everyone obeyed this law, for the practice was soon back in London after the Restoration of the monarchy. From Samuel Pepys' diary entries from the 1660s, we learn that both married and single people drew lots, men as well as women. This meant that people often had two Valentines—the person they had drawn and the person who had drawn them (within a generation this had changed and only men drew names). On February 16, 1667, Pepys wrote of the newest Valentine's Day fad, that of drawing mottoes along with names:

> *I find that Mrs. Pierce's little girl is my Valentine, she having drawn me, which I am not sorry for, it easing me of something more I must have given to others. But I do first observe the fashion of drawing mottoes as well as names; so that Pierce, who drew my wife, did also draw a motto, and this girl drew another for me. What mine was I have forgot; but My wife's was, 'Most courteous and most fair'; which as it may be used, or an anagram made upon each name, might be very pretty.*

This fad appears not to have caught on and quickly fell into disuse.

A unique variation to the custom of drawing lots was practiced in the county of Derbyshire. If a girl's boyfriend did not visit her or give her a kiss on Valentine's Day, she was declared by the other women to be "dusty" and was brushed off with brooms. After this, the girl had to draw lots for Valentines with everyone else.

Scotland

The earliest mention of the custom of drawing lots for Valentines in Scotland is found in the poem "For His Valentine" by the Scottish poet William Fowler (d. 1612). In the poem, Fowler writes of drawing a woman's name and then asking the woman for some small gift or token to show that she finds him acceptable as a Valentine. If he does not receive the required favor, he will burn the paper with her name on it and curse the saint—being Protestant, Fowler did not recognize the saints and did not consider it a blasphemy to curse them.

The custom of drawing the name of one's Valentine was done with a unique twist along the Scottish border. Each person selected a slip three times, returning the slip after each of the first two draws. If a person drew the same name all three times, it was a sign that the individual drawn was a future spouse. In some areas, the guy would then take the slip of paper with the girl's name written on it to her house and would receive an apple or other treat in return.

DID YOU KNOW?

The custom of drawing names for Valentines was also practiced in some parts of France. The bishop Francis de Sales (1567–1622) disapproved of the custom and sought to eliminate it or, at the very least, to change it. He tried to get people to draw the names of saints to especially honor in the coming year instead. His efforts came to naught, and young men continued to draw the names of eligible young women.

The First Person I See Must My True Love Be

In England, there was another method for choosing Valentines besides drawing lots: the first non-relative a person saw on Valentine's Day was supposed to be one's Valentine for the next year. Like drawing lots, this practice was supposed to be entirely random, but not everyone was content to leave something as important as choosing a Valentine up to chance. Choosing Valentines was often part of courting, and people who were Valentines (whether by drawing lots, by choice or by being the first person seen on Valentine's Day) sometimes did eventually marry. This custom was especially common in the western part of England.

In 1633, a Dutch visitor to London described it so:

> ...it is customary, alike for married as for unmarried
> people, that the first person one meets in the morning,
> that is, if one is a man, the first woman or girl,
> becomes one's Valentine. He asks her name which he
> takes down and carries on a long strip of paper in his
> hat band, and in the same way the woman or girl
> wears his name on her bodice; but it is the practice that
> they meet on the evening before and choose each other
> for their Valentine, and, come Easter, they send each
> other gloves, silk stockings, or sometimes a miniature
> portrait, which the ladies wear to foster the friendship.

People who followed this custom frequently tried to rig the
results. For example, the wife of Samuel Pepys was careful not
to look at any of the men painting their chimney in 1662 so
as to ensure that one Will Bowyer would be her Valentine that
year. Some people walked blindfolded to the home of their
beloved to ensure they got the Valentine they wanted. In Sir
Walter Scott's novel *The Fair Maid of Perth*, Henry Gow rises
early in the morning to walk to Catherine Glover's house in the
hopes that he will be the first man she sees on Valentine's Day
and will thus become her Valentine.

Thee first I spyed, and the first swain we see,
In spite of fortune, shall our true-love be.

–female narrator in John Gay's
"Shepherd's Week" (1714)

Valentine's Day Customs from Norfolk

The eastern English county of Norfolk has a long and colorful history of celebrating St. Valentine's Day. Indeed, the earliest known Valentine's love letters in the country were those exchanged between the Norfolk couple Margery Brews and John Paston in February 1477 (see page 26).

It is known that by the late 18th century, children in Norfolk went out early on Valentine's morning collecting pennies and treats. The children would rise very early and go about demanding a Valentine from any adults they encountered. It was important to get an early start because once the sun had risen, they would be told that they had been sunburned and would no longer be given any treats.

Upon encountering an adult or knocking on someone's door, the children would cry "Good morrow, Valentine!" before the adult could speak, thereby entitling them to a reward. In Ryburgh, the verse the children sang was "God bless the baker, / If you will be the giver, / I will be the maker." In a 1773 diary entry, Parson James Woodforde of Weston Longville noted that he had given each child in his parish under the age of 14 a penny for Valentine's Day.

This custom was still being practiced in early 20th-century Norwich. Children went to the homes of the well-to-do to beg for money on Valentine's Day. The rich folks would heat up the halfpennies over the fire and then toss them out onto the road. The heat made the coins difficult to grasp, adding to the fun.

Another Norfolk Valentine's custom is the giving of anonymous gifts, which is still done today. Packages full of sweets are placed on doorsteps on the evening of February 13. The giver, known as Jack Valentine, rings the doorbell and then flees before someone opens the door. Children have traditionally been the recipients of these gifts, with their parents generally being the givers. However, sometimes adults also are happily surprised to hear their doorbells ring. Occasionally an extra bit of fun is added by tying a string to the package and pulling it away when the recipient reaches for it, making them chase after the present; this is known as a snatch Valentine.

Unfortunately, there are always some mean-spirited people who have to put a damper on things. A nasty twist to the Jack Valentine custom is to leave a large package filled with nothing more than a cruel verse on a person's doorstep.

Rhyming in Oxfordshire of Old

In 19th-century Oxfordshire, it was customary for children to go begging for treats on Valentine's Day. The children either went door to door to houses or businesses, or they stopped whomever they saw on the road. Each community seems to have had its own rhyme that the children would sing to ask for a small gift of some sort. Here are some of them:

> *"Good morrow, Valentine,*
> *I'll be yours if you'll be mine,*
> *Good morrow, Valentine."*

(from Charlbury)

> *"The Rose is red, the violet's blue,*
> *The carnation's sweet, and so are you.*
> *And so are they that sent you this,*
> *And when we meet we'll have a kiss."*

(from the Baldons)

> *"The rose is red, the violet's blue*
> *The carnation's sweet, and so be you,*
> *So please to give us a Valentine."*

(from Bodicote)

If no treat was given, the children cried out, "The devil's black and so be you!"

Each community had its own traditional gifts, as well. In Lower Heyford, the children received nuts or small cakes. In Shipton, chocolate was distributed. In Chipping Norton, the local business owners gave out the treats, which in this case were halfpennies. The sole exception was the baker, who gave buns instead.

More of Cupid's Customs

♥ It was an old English custom for girls to sit cross-legged and pray to St. Valentine for good luck in love.

💜 A very unusual tradition from western England involved catching birds in a net. Three young men would take a clap-net on Valentine's Day and try to catch an owl and two sparrows in it. If successful, the men were treated to three pots of purl by every house in the area at which they claimed their prize. Apparently, the purpose of the exercise was to show that it was good for couples to get tied up together, so to speak. The sparrows represented a young couple while the owl symbolized the wisdom of the ages.

💜 In Rutland, children went door to door collecting Valentine's buns on February 14. In Northumberland, children received these treats from their godparents on the Sundays before and after Valentine's Day. Valentine's buns were sweet currant buns twisted into the shape of a heart.

💜 In Buckinghamshire, a person would approach a member of the opposite sex on Valentine's Day and recite, "Good morrow to you, Valentine, / First 'tis yours and then 'tis mine, / I'll thank you for a Valentine."

💜 Boys in Worcestershire used to go from house to house begging for apples on Valentine's Day. These they would take home, where their mothers would cut them up and use them to make fritters for everyone.

💜 In Berkshire, children sang this rhyme while begging for treats on Valentine's Day: "Knock the kettle against the pan, / Give us a penny if you can / We be ragged and you be fine, / Please to give us a Valentine. / Up with the kettle, down with the spout, / Give us a penny and we'll get out."

💜 In villages in Hertfordshire, the children would gather together on the morning of Valentine's Day and visit the homes of the well-to-do, who would shower them with flowers. The girls then wove them into garlands and draped them over the shoulders and arms of one of the youngest boys. The whole group then went about the village singing, "Good morrow to you, Valentine; / Curl your locks as I do mine, / Two before and three behind, / Good morrow to you, Valentine," and got halfpennies.

❤ In the 1830s, at Ecton, Northamptonshire, children got straight to the point on Valentine's Day, chanting, "Morrow, morrow, Valentine, / Empty your purse and fill mine."

❤ In the Victorian period, a popular Valentine's Day game for children was "Drop the Handkerchief." A girl would drop her handkerchief near a boy she liked. He then had to chase her to claim his kiss.

A Courting Custom

It did not take long for Valentine's Day to become part of the courting ritual in England and later elsewhere. Men used this day of love to reveal their affection, to advance a relationship or to "seal the deal" with a marriage proposal or even a wedding. A woman, too, could take advantage of the opportunity to attract the attention of the man she fancied.

A Helping Hand

Elias Ashmole (1617–1692), the antiquarian whose collection provided the foundation for Oxford's Ashmolean Museum, was courting Mary, Lady Manwaring in 1647. When the lady's interest in him increased in mid-February, he attributed it to the power of Valentine's Day. Whether it was the magic of the day or something else, the couple eventually wed in 1649. She was 20 years his senior. It was his second marriage, her fourth.

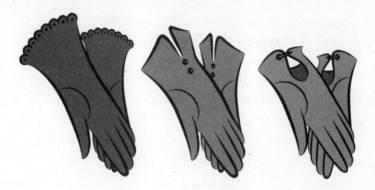

I (G)love You!

Gloves were once a popular courtship and Valentine's Day gift. They often took the place of an engagement ring. The 1684 *Poor Robin's Almanac* noted that on February 14 milliners would do brisk sales in ribbons and gloves. The diarist Samuel Pepys left behind several Valentine's Day entries that reveal that gloves were a common gift at the time. On February 18, 1661, he wrote:

> *In the afternoon, my wife and I and Miss Martha Batten, my Valentine, to the Exchange, and there, upon a payre of embroidered and six payre of plain white gloves, I laid out 40s. upon her.*

Gloves remained a popular gift into the Victorian period. In late 19th-century Devonshire, it was customary to give one's Valentine a pair of gloves. Paper hands were also given as love tokens and appeared frequently on Victorian-era Valentines. The reason is likely connected to the notion of asking for a woman's hand in marriage.

Gloves were not the only gift to give one's Valentine. Samuel Pepys also mentions silk stockings as common gifts to give those in his social circle. When his Valentine was from a lower echelon of society, a coin or two sufficed. In recording the gift-giving practices of the nobility, Pepys recorded that costly gifts of jewels were expected. For example, in 1667, Lord Mandeville gave the Duchess of Richmond a ring valued at £300, a small fortune at the time. On a previous Valentine's Day, the same duchess had drawn the name of the Duke of York as her Valentine and received a ring worth £800. In contrast, the ring Pepys intended as a Valentine's Day gift for his wife in 1668 cost about £5. Clearly the means and social status of both the giver and the recipient were important; appearances needed to be kept.

This month bright Phoebus enters Pisces,
The maids will have good store of kisses,
For always when the fun comes there,
Valentine's Day is drawing near,
And both the men and maids incline
To chuse them each a Valentine;
And if a man gets one he loves,
He gives her first a pair of gloves;
And, by the way, remember this,
To seal the favour with a kiss.
This kiss begets more love, and then
That love begets a kiss again,
Until this trade the man doth catch,
And then he doth propose the match.
The woman's willing, tho' she's shy,
She gives the man this soft reply,
"I'll not resolve one thing or other,
Until I first consult my mother."
When she says so, 'tis half a grant,
And may be taken for consent.

–from *Poor Robin's Almanac* (1757)

Welsh Love Spoons

Since the 17th century, young Welsh men have taken the time to carve fancy spoons full of elaborate designs for the women they loved and hoped to marry. Originally, these spoons had nothing to do with Valentine's Day but were simply an important part of the culture's courting customs. The spoon designs were replete with a variety of symbols that conveyed to the woman the man's hopes and dreams for their future together. The spoon itself showed that the man would provide food for the woman and any children born to the couple. The carving also showed the man's skills as a handyman. As Valentine's Day became more widely celebrated in Wales (and now with St. Dwynwen's Day in January, as well), the giving of love spoons naturally migrated to this time of the year for many people.

Today, men can buy an already carved love spoon online or in a store. However, carving the spoon themselves makes the gift extra special and adds so much meaning. A simple spoon is not overly difficult to carve. Here is a guide to the symbols most often found on these spoons:

- ♥ Heart = love. Two hearts, as in a double love spoon, often means a commitment has already been made between the couple.

- ♥ Birds = love birds.

- ♥ Keys = the keys to his heart.

- ♥ Bells = the desire to marry.

- ♥ Harp = harmony. It is also a symbol for Wales.

- ♥ Dragon = protection. It, too, is a symbol for Wales.

- ♥ Shield = protection.

- ♥ Horseshoe = hope for good fortune in their relationship.

- ❤ Diamond = hope for wealth.

- ❤ Anchor = steadfastness. Sailors generally included an anchor or some other nautical symbol on the love spoons they carved.

- ❤ Spade = willingness to work hard.

- ❤ Cross = faith, religion.

- ❤ Balls in a cage = a desire for children. The number of balls indicated how many children he wanted to have.

- ❤ Chain links = a desire for children. Each link represented a child.

- ❤ Fruit = fruitfulness.

- ❤ Tree = strength and fertility.

Love spoons, which were also found in other parts of Europe, are thought to be where the term "spooning" originated. In Wales, *spooner* is an old word for "boyfriend."

DID YOU KNOW?

A Welsh folk belief was that a baby born on Valentine's Day would have many lovers.

Lovestruck

The earliest known Valentine from what is now Canada dates back to 1784 in Nova Scotia. The poem asked the recipient, Amelia DesBarres, to help the sender to become a better man. We know of the Valentine because the sender's sister, Rebecca Byles, copied it in a letter sent to her aunt in Boston, whom she informed that her brother was behaving like a lovesick fool.

No popular respect will I omit
To do thee honor on this happy day,
When every loyal lover tasks his wit
His simple truth in studious rhymes to pay,
And to his mistress dear his hopes convey.
Rather thou knowest I would still outrun
All calendars with Love's,—whose date alway
Thy bright eyes govern better than the Sun,—
For with thy favor was my life begun;
And still I reckon on from smiles to smiles,
And not by summers, for I thrive on none
But those thy cheerful countenance complies:
Oh! if it be to choose and call thee mine,
Love, thou art every day my Valentine.

–Thomas Hood (1799–1845),
"Sonnet for the 14th of February"

Who Will My True Love Be?

Everyone wants to find their true love. Prior to the 20th century, however, marrying was one of a woman's few options, so the quest for a husband was the focus of many women's attention. Divorce was rare and difficult to attain, so every young woman prayed to find a man who would treat her well. In "Pairing Time Anticipated," the English poet and hymn writer William Cowper (1731–1800) warns against choosing a life partner too soon (e.g., before St. Valentine's Day) and prematurely marrying. In the time before divorce was common, a hasty marriage could lead to a lifetime of regret.

Single women (and sometimes bachelors, as well) participated in a variety of fun superstitions to try to catch a glimpse of their futures. These little rituals were often carried out on holidays, such as Valentine's Day. Here are some superstitions and customs from England and New England.

♥ A young woman would write the names of several young men on individual pieces of paper and wrap these in balls of clay. The balls were then dropped in a bowl of water. The first ball to rise to the top contained the name of the woman's Valentine and future husband.

♥ A young woman would pin a bay leaf to each corner of her pillow and one in the center. The man she dreamt of that night would be her Valentine.

♥ A young woman would remove the yolk from a hard-boiled egg and replace it with salt. She ate the egg right before going to bed and drank nothing afterward. The man she dreamt of was her Valentine.

♥ A woman who saw a squirrel on Valentine's Day knew she would marry a man who would hoard away all their money.

♥ A woman who found a man's glove on Valentine's Day had only to find the owner to meet her future husband.

♥ The first bird a woman saw flying overhead on Valentine's Day would tell her about her future husband. A sparrow meant that the woman's husband would be a farmer; a robin indicated a sailor and a blackbird a clergyman. A goldfinch was a sign that her husband would be rich. A dove meant he would be a good husband while a crossbill was a sign that he would be a bad-tempered fellow. A woodpecker indicated that the woman would never marry.

♥ If a woman ran around the local church 12 times reciting a special verse at midnight on St. Valentine's Eve and then returned home to sleep with a sprig of rosemary under her pillow, she would dream of her future husband. This custom was also practiced by Hungarian women.

♥ In Derbyshire, young women would look through the key-hole of the door before leaving the house on Valentine's Day. If a girl saw a hen and rooster together, it meant she was destined to marry that year.

♥ In Devonshire, a girl who wanted to know the identity of her future husband would go to the churchyard and, at half past midnight, walk home. On her way, she would see her future husband behind her, raking into a winding sheet (used for burial before coffins were common).

💜 A young man might twist the stem of an apple on Valentine's Day while reciting the names of various women. The name he was saying when the stem finally broke would be the name of his future wife.

💜 During the mid-20th century, girls counted the buttons on their clothes on Valentine's Day to see who they would marry: "rich man, poor man, beggar man, thief, doctor, lawyer, merchant, chief."

💜 If a woman saw another woman first on the morning of Valentine's Day, she would not marry that year. But if she saw a man first, she would.

💜 Single women wore a crocus in a buttonhole on Valentine's Day to increase the likelihood that they would meet their true love that day.

💜 In Oxfordshire, if a dark-skinned man walked by the house of an unmarried girl on Valentine's Day, she would marry within the year.

Young people in other areas also tried to determine their future marital happiness at this time of year.

💜 A Hungarian woman believed that if she dreamt of birds on Valentine's night, she would marry within the year.

💜 Single Hungarian women would not do any sweeping after sunset on Valentine's Day because to do so would mean they would never marry.

💜 Hungarian newlyweds joined hands on Valentine's Day and had both their mothers wash their hands with holy water. The holy water was then poured over the couple's heads. This ritual was supposed to keep them safe from harm.

♥ Young German girls would plant onions on Valentine's Day, placing the name of a man they knew beside each bulb. The name closest to the first bulb to sprout would be that of their future husband.

Other Valentine's Day Folk Customs and Beliefs

♥ In the Ozark Mountains in the U.S., it is customary to plant lettuce on February 14.

♥ In Tennessee, it is traditional to plant garden peas on Valentine's Day.

♥ In Poland, it was believed that wheat grew best if it was planted before sunset on St. Valentine's Day.

♥ In eastern England, it was formerly believed that Valentine's Day was a good time for the preparation of eels for the purposes of magic.

♥ In Slovenia, St. Valentine's Day (known as St. Zdravko's Day) was the best time to start work in the fields and vineyards.

♥ One Hungarian folk belief about February 14 is that if Valentine's Day (known as St. Bálint's Day) is cold and dry, there will be a good harvest in the fall.

♥ In Topolya, Hungary, wind on Valentine's Day meant that the chickens would not lay many eggs.

♥ In the village of Cserszegtomaj, Hungary, farmers walk around the edges of their fields and vineyards before sunset on St. Valentine's Day in the belief that it will protect their crops from birds and thieves.

♥ In Wales, it was believed that a calf born on February 14 would be useless for breeding.

- ♥ Another Welsh folk belief about St. Valentine's Day was that any eggs laid by the hens on that day would be rotten.

- ♥ In Warwickshire and Huntingdonshire, it was customary to begin bean planting on St. Valentine's Day. All bean seeds needed to be in the ground by St. Benedict's Day on March 21.

- ♥ Cambridgeshire farmers judged whether or not it was a good year to grow peas by the amount of dew present on Valentine's morning. A lot of dew meant it would be a good year for peas.

- ♥ In Wales it was thought that bringing snowdrops into a house on Valentine's Day foretold the death of a member of the household in the coming year.

DID YOU  **KNOW?**

Groundhog Day was originally held on February 14.

The Erotic Side of Love

"The Choise of Valentines" (or "Nashe's Dildo") is an erotic poem written in 1592 or 1593 by Thomas Nashe (b. 1567), an English poet and playwright. Nashe was a writer often embroiled in controversies. His only known foray into writing erotica was no exception. Nashe had never intended the poem to have a large audience, and it was distributed only in manuscript form to select individuals. It was dedicated to "Lord S," thought to be either Ferdinando Stanley, fifth earl of Derby, or Henry Wriothesley, third earl of Southampton. Its content, however, made it difficult for the poem to be kept a secret, and it created quite a stir.

The poem was first published in 1899, and today, six different versions are in existence. The general plot centers upon a Valentine's Day encounter in a brothel. Tomalin, the protagonist, travels into the countryside to locate his old sweetheart only to discover that she has moved to London and is working as a prostitute. Making his way back to the capital, Tomalin finds the brothel and his old flame, Frances. Anxious to celebrate Valentine's Day with her, Tomalin is embarrassed when he loses his erection upon lifting her skirts. Frances lends him a helping hand, and things proceed as planned until Tomalin reaches the high point in the couple's festivities before Frances does. Momentarily disappointed, Frances quickly takes matters into her own hands with a little help from a bedside companion.

"The Choise of Valentines" contains the earliest known use of the term "dildo" in Renaissance literature. It is quite explicit, with a large section devoted to a description of Frances' second choice as a Valentine's Day companion (i.e., her dildo).

DID YOU KNOW?

Just over 400 years after Nashe wrote his erotic poem, a different solution to Tomalin's original problem with Frances was discovered—Viagra. Pfizer, the makers of this miraculous little blue pill, funded an Impotence Awareness Day in Great Britain on Valentine's Day 2000. Two years later, on February 13, 2002, radio ads in New York City told men there was still time to obtain Viagra for Valentine's Day. All they had to do was visit a certain website and get an online prescription.

MESSAGES OF LOVE: ALL ABOUT VALENTINE'S DAY CARDS

Valentine's Cards

The practice of giving cards on Valentine's Day grew out of the European custom of visiting friends on New Year's Day and leaving a calling card. By the 1770s, specially crafted Valentine's calling cards were in use in Germany and France. By the 1780s, they were in use in England.

Prior to this time, the odd card had been made as a gift. A very early mention of such a gift is found in the diary of the 17th-century English civil servant Samuel Pepys (1633–1703) in his entry for February 14, 1667: "This morning come up to my wife's bedside—I being up and dressing myself—little Will Mercer to be her Valentine; and brought her name writ upon blue paper in gold letters, done by himself, very pretty, and we were both well pleased with it."

Valentine Writers

At first, people had to make their own Valentine's cards—not an easy task in a period when fancy craft materials were not available. Then someone came up with the idea of selling booklets of love poems that could be copied onto handmade cards. These "Valentine Writers" that first appeared in the market in the late 18th century were quite popular, judging from the frequency with which some of their verses appear in contemporary Valentines.

Valentine Writers contained both sentimental and satiric verses. There were declarations of love as well as a selection of responses from which to choose. The romantic verses cited not just the joys of being in love but the pains, as well. The earliest Valentine Writers contained verses appropriate to various classes, ages and qualities (e.g., beauty and wit). Many of the verses were written in such a way that the sender could easily modify them to better suit the recipient. In the following example from "Hymen's Revenge" (c. 1805, London), the color of the beloved's hair could easily be changed:

> Hard to describe those matchless charms,
> Which long I've wish'd within my arms,
> Yet I'll attempt—thy nut brown hair,
> Thy skin, like snow white lilies fair;
> Thy taper fingers and thy waiste,
> By Venus self can't be surpas't...thou are half divine,
> Dearest, do let me call thee mine.

The poems were adequate for the occasion, like most Valentine's poems, but were certainly no literary masterpieces. Nonetheless, many women kept the Valentine's cards they received for years to come, often for the rest of their lives.

Manufactured Valentine's Cards and the Penny Post

By 1809, the first printed Valentine's cards were being sold. In England, Doblis & Company was the earliest noteworthy manufacturer of these cards. The New York City firm of Elton & Co. claimed to be the first American manufacturer of Valentine's cards—probably starting in the mid-1830s. By the 1870s, commercial Valentines had largely replaced handmade ones.

The trend of sending Valentine's cards caught on quickly and spread rapidly. It is estimated that by the 1820s, 200,000 Valentine's cards were being exchanged yearly in the city of London. Within two decades that amount had doubled. Then in 1840, something happened in Great Britain that revolutionized the sending of Valentine's cards—the Penny Post was introduced.

The Penny Post was revolutionary because it standardized the amount of postage paid regardless of the distance the item was traveling. Prior to this event, the farther the letter/card/package was being sent, the more postage it cost. The expense severely reduced the exchange of Valentine's cards and letters between rural folks and people who had moved to the city. In 1840, this barrier was lifted and the results were immediate. By 1855, an estimated 800,000 Valentine's cards were being sent in the mail. By 1867, the number had reached one million; by 1882, one-and-a-half million.

When the U.S. followed suit and introduced the Penny Post in 1845, the amount of Valentine's cards sent also rose quickly there. Indeed, between the 1840s and the 1860s, postmen in major American cities were forced to use wheelbarrows to cart all the Valentine's cards they had to deliver, while extra staff was hired to help sort all the cards. English essayist and author Charles Lamb (1775–1834) expressed his sympathy for the postmen on this day: "The weary and all for-spent twopenny postman sinks beneath a load of embarrassments not his own. It is scarcely credible to what extent this ephemeral courtship is carried on in this loving town, to the great enrichment of porters, and detriment of knockers and bell-wires."

On February 14 in 19th-century England, women anxiously awaited the postman and the delivery of Valentines. If no cards were received, it was particularly painful because all the neighbors would have observed his lack of delivery. The poem in Tom Hood's *Comic Annual* for February 1835 describes the attempts made by a woman to attract a suitor and the suicidal despair she feels when on Valentine's Day her neighbor receives several Valentines via the post while she herself receives none.

Not everyone approved of this new fad of buying and sending Valentine's cards. Critics of Valentine's Day in 19th-century North America described the new practice as vulgar and irreligious. Many Victorians feared that the commercialization of Valentine's Day would lead to a loss of sincerity in courtship. Critics claimed store-bought Valentines actually disconnected people from their emotions and from other people, the opposite of what Valentines and love tokens were intended to do. The American poet and essayist Ralph Waldo Emerson (1803–1882) was a critic and opponent of manufactured Valentines.

Retailers pushed Valentine's Day into prominence in 19th-century America in order to increase revenue. During the 1850s, American retailers turned Valentine's Day into a week- or month-long celebration. By the mid-19th century, Valentines were also being sold to give to friends and relatives. Victorian retailers tried to sell the magical effects of sending Valentines, claiming they were a necessary part of courtship. Special leap year Valentines were introduced, which were meant to be sent by women to men—an inversion of the normal ritual.

Proponents of the practice of exchanging Valentine's cards believed that it helped some people to overcome obstacles to courtship, such as shyness or geographical distance. It was argued that commercial Valentine's cards made it easier for less creative individuals to participate and also made it easier for women to express their romantic interest.

By the start of the 20th century, the custom of exchanging Valentine's cards was dying out in England. Indeed, in her 1913 book *Rustic Speech and Folklore*, Elizabeth Mary Wright wrote, "The custom of writing and of sending Valentines is out of fashion and there remains little to mark the day." Then in 1925, Lady Jeanetta Tuck suggested a revival of these love notes as a way of commemorating her husband Sir Adolph Tuck's greeting card firm's 60th anniversary. The cards were a success, and the tradition was revived.

The practice of exchanging Valentine's cards had never died out in the U.S. Children exchanged Valentine's cards with their classmates—a practice that remains common today. In fact, teachers receive more Valentine's cards than anyone else. School-aged children are a close second, followed by mothers and wives.

At present, over a billion Valentine's cards are sold annually in the U.S., with Valentine's Day being the second most popular day to exchange cards (Christmas being the most popular).

Sure, of all days that ever were dated,
Valentine's Day is the fullest of news;
Then every lass expects to be mated
And Cupid goes round collecting his dues!
And levies a door-rate, like parish or poor-rate,
By getting the Postman to stand in his shoes.

–Thomas Hood (1799–1845), "Valentine's Day"

Types of Valentine's Cards

Puzzle Purse Valentines
One of the earliest types of Valentine's card was the puzzle purse Valentine. These cards were difficult to construct and took a lot of creativity and patience. They were designed to fold up in a complex pattern that, when unfolded, revealed a pretty design as well as verses that were meant to be read in a certain order. Several handmade examples of these cards exist from the 18th century. By the mid-19th century, this type of Valentine's card had become quite popular. The cards sometimes opened to reveal a tiny gift, such as a lock of hair.

My dear the heart which you behold
Will break when you the same unfold.
Even so my heart with lovesick pain
Sure wounded is and breaks in twain.

(from a puzzle purse Valentine, 1790)

Acrostic Valentines

An acrostic poem is one in which the first letter of each line spells out a word; in the case of a Valentine's acrostic, the name of the beloved is spelled out. An example of such a Valentine is the poem written on February 14, 1846, by Virginia Poe for her husband, the famous poet and author Edgar Allan Poe:

> *Ever with thee I wish to roam—*
> *Dearest my life is thine.*
> *Give me a cottage for my home*
> *And a rich old cypress vine,*
> *Removed from the world with its sin and care*
> *And the tattling of many tongues.*
> *Love alone shall guide us when we are there—*
> *Love shall heal my weakened lungs;*
> *And Oh, the tranquil hours we'll spend,*
> *Never wishing that others may see!*
> *Perfect ease we'll enjoy, without thinking to lend*
> *Ourselves to the world and its glee—*
> *Ever peaceful and blissful we'll be.*

DID YOU  KNOW?

Edgar Allan Poe also wrote an acrostic Valentine in 1846. "For Her This Rhyme Is Penned" was published in the *New York Evening Mirror*. The woman's name was Frances Sargent Osgoode, a fellow poet who, like Poe, was married. The exact nature of their close relationship is not clear, but Poe's wife is known to have encouraged it because of its positive effects on her husband. Poe's acrostic Valentine is somewhat atypical in that the recipient's name is not spelled from the first letter of each line but from the first letter in line one, the second letter in line two, the third in line three, etc.

Rebus Valentines

Sometimes the messages in Valentines were written in a combination of words and pictures. The recipient had to substitute words for the pictures in order to read the message. This type of Valentine was known as a rebus Valentine. An example is:

> *You are the ☼ and the ☾ and the ✦ to me.*
> *I ♥ you.*

Fraktur Valentines

A Fraktur Valentine was one where the message was written in an older style of lettering. The message was typically surrounded with hand-drawn pictures. Birds and roses were popular images. These Valentines resembled illuminated medieval manuscripts. Such Valentines were popular in Pennsylvania, where they grew out of the custom of the German settlers known as the Pennsylvania Dutch for producing elaborately lettered and beautifully decorated birth and marriage certificates.

Pinprick Valentines

Pinprick Valentines looked like lace. To make them, tiny holes were poked into a sheet of paper using either a pin or a needle. To cover an entire sheet of paper with these little holes was a long and painstakingly tedious process. Going to such effort was something that a person did only for someone very special.

Pinprick Valentines originated in the convents of 16th-century France and the Holy Roman Empire. Nuns made sheets of this paper lace and decorated each one with a religious image or a heart. The sheets were then sold and the proceeds used for charitable purposes. The people who bought these sheets of paper lace often gave them as gifts on special occasions, including Valentine's Day.

In 1834, Joseph Addenbrooke accidentally filed off some raised embossed paper, thereby creating a quicker and easier way to make paper lace. He worked for the English firm of Dobbs, which then began to manufacture paper lace.

DID YOU  KNOW?

Envelopes originally needed to be folded and sealed with wax. Wafers of wax with specially designed images or mottoes were available to purchase in the early 19th century for sending Valentines.

Cut-out Valentines

Similar to paper lace Valentines but far less delicate were the cut-out Valentines. A piece of paper was folded several times and then shapes were cut out. When the paper was unfolded, a lovely design was revealed. This method is the same one that children are often taught to make snowflakes in art class.

Four hearts in one you do behold,
& they in Each other do infold,
I Cut them out on such a Night,
& send them to my hearts delight,
On such A Night the hour of Nine,
I Chuse you for my valintine,
I Chuse you out from all the rest,
The reason is I liked you best,
Some draw Valentines by lotts,
Some draw them that they love not,
But I draw you wich I do Chuse,
I hope you will not refuse,
My heart within by Breast doth Ake,
A Tonge I have but dare not speak,
If I should speak & should not speed,
Then my poor heart will break indeed.

(from a cut-out Valentine, Pennsylvania, 1799)

Theorem Valentines

Theorem Valentines (also known as Poonah Valentines) were
made using stenciled images. The idea of cutting images into
oiled paper and then using this paper to paint that image onto
an object was created in Asia and brought back to Europe by
merchants. After the image was painted onto the sheet of paper,
a coat of gum Arabic (a substance made from the sap of acacia
trees) was painted over top to keep the paint from running.

Window and Beehive Valentines

Both window and beehive Valentines are ones with hidden pictures. With a window Valentine, the picture is hidden under-
neath a flap. The beehive Valentine (also sometimes referred to
as a flower or cobweb Valentine) consisted of a picture cut into
paper threads which, when lifted by an attached string, revealed
another hidden picture.

Mechanical Valentines

German manufacturers began to make Valentine's cards with moveable parts in the 1890s, which they exported to other countries. Mechanical Valentines did not really catch on in the U.S. until the 1920s. In 1927, the Beistle Company became the first American manufacturer to produce such cards, followed soon after by the Auburn Post Card Company, Louis Katz of New York, Carrington Company of Chicago, the Rochester Lithograph Company and Steiner Litho Co. Germany and the United States produced mechanical Valentines until World War II. After the war, the preference was for the less expensive, non-moveable cards.

The card manufacturers used a variety of ways to make the parts move. Some Valentines had a string fastened to a part like an arm or a wing, which would then wave or flap when pulled. Other Valentines accomplished the same thing by inserting a paper tab that was either pulled in and out or up and down. Various types of metal fasteners were used to join separate parts, such as wheels, which were then moveable.

Postcard Valentines

Picture postcards were introduced from Europe to England in 1894 and the U.S. in 1897 and quickly became all the rage. Many Valentines from this time were postcards. The majority were produced in Germany.

DID YOU KNOW?

One 19th-century Valentine looked so much like real currency that it was pulled from the shelves in Britain.

Early Valentine's Card Manufacturers

England

♥ John Gregory Hancock was the first manufacturer of embossed paper in England in 1796.

♥ The early 19th-century London company of H. Dobbs & Co. was the first to put delicate paper petals on Valentines, which could be lifted to reveal a hidden message.

♥ By the 1850s, there were 13 paper lace makers in England. The most successful was Joseph Mansell.

♥ The largest manufacturer of Valentines in England in the second half of the 19th century was Jonathon King. King got his start working for the fancy paper manufacturer Dobbs. So important were these love tokens to his business that he named his fourteenth child Sydney Valentine King.

♥ Jonathon King was a great collector of Valentine's cards and is responsible for the survival of the majority of Victorian-era Valentines still around today.

♥ Walter Crane (1845–1915) and Kate Greenaway (1846–1901) were two Victorian artists who drew greeting cards to supplement their incomes. Both drew cards for the British manufacturer Marcus Ward and Company.

♥ In 1876, Marcus Ward and Company combined eight Valentines drawn by Crane and Greenaway into a book called *The Quiver of Love*. Crane disliked the book.

♥ Cracker-like Valentines were marketed by a London merchant in 1846.

♥ In the 1860s, Eugene Rimmel, a perfumier, began marketing scented sachet Valentines. The fancy decorated envelopes were stuffed with scented cotton. Rimmel employed 80 to 100 women to make the sachets.

♥ Thomas Stevens, an English manufacturer from Coventry, introduced silk Valentine bookmarks in the 1860s and 1870s.

<h2>DID YOU  KNOW?</h2>

Despite the fantastic success of the Valentines she drew, Kate Greenaway never received more than about £3 per design.

United States: Howland and Whitney

Esther Howland (1828–1904) was the daughter of a stationer from Worcester, Massachusetts. She attended Mount Holyoke Women's Seminary, where the founder, Mary Lyon, did not allow the students to participate in the new Valentine's festivities, though some students did on the sly. One day, after graduating, Howland saw some fancy English Valentines her father had imported. Howland decided to make some of her own with ribbons and lace. Her brother took the cards with him on a sales trip. He sold them all and received orders for more that totaled $5000—a fortune in those days. Howland hired several women to help her make Valentines in an assembly line-style of production in her father's house.

Eventually, the business became so big that a separate building was purchased for it. Howland established the New England Valentine Company in the early 1870s. The company grossed over $100,000 a year, and Howland passed some of these huge profits to her employees by paying them very well for the time. Howland's cards were marked with a tiny red "H" in the corner.

George C. Whitney (1842–1915) of the company of that name bought Howland's business in the early 1880s when Howland's father became ill and she chose to devote herself to nursing him. Whitney disliked the mean, humorous Valentines known as "vinegar Valentines" and refused to produce them. As his company became one of the largest greeting card companies in the country, this dislike played a large role in the decline of the cruel Valentines.

From the 1890s onward, the Whitney firm specialized in children's Valentines. It also made special ones for teachers. The company also produced heart-shaped Valentines; previously, all Valentines had been a standard rectangular shape. Whitney's company was the largest American card manufacturing company before it closed in 1942. At its peak it employed 150 people full-time and another 450 on a seasonal basis.

Words that are fond
Words that are true
In truth and love
I offer you.

(from an Esther Howland Valentine's card,
19th century)

Vinegar Valentines

Around the 1840s, cruel anti-Valentines began to be produced and sold. These insulting Valentines were known as "vinegar Valentines." Anti-Valentines were not new; satiric verses had been included in early Valentine Writers. However, now that they were available pre-made, they became much more common. Indeed, by the 1850s, many firms emphasized the vinegar Valentines because they were cheaper to make and had a larger market. In his *Book of Days* (1863), Robert Chambers opined that vinegar Valentines were more popular than sentimental ones, an opinion held by many people by the 1880s.

Many vinegar Valentines included an unflattering caricature image of the recipient, along with a derogatory verse. Others contained just the picture, which was insulting enough.

Vinegar Valentines were a new sort of charivari, an attempt to keep everyone in their places in a society changing at an unprecedented rate. The development and expansion of a middle class disrupted the ages-old duality of only an upper and lower class. Vinegar Valentines helped to mark the shifting boundaries of the new middle class and were especially popular from the mid-19th to early 20th centuries.

These mock Valentines, given to those who did not conform to communal norms, were usually sent anonymously. In the early days of the postal system, it was doubly insulting to receive a rude Valentine in the mail because the recipient had to pay the postage.

The earliest vinegar Valentines attacked a person's social or marital status. For example, a man who waited to gain his fortune before marrying was ridiculed in one verse:

> *You nasty old bachelor, sad and forlorn,*
> *I fear all the ladies will treat you with scorn;*
> *In vain now you'd wed, when your locks are*
> *like snow,*
> *But maids in derision, cry, "No, my love, no."*

Other verses frequently focused on a person's profession. An individual's character, personality and appearance were always open to criticism. Vinegar Valentines were also popular responses to undesirable suitors:

> *I'm not attracted by your glitter,*
> *For well I know how very bitter*
> *My life would be, if I should take*
> *You for my spouse, a rattlesnake.*
> *Oh no, I'd not accept the ring,*
> *Or evermore 'twould prove a sting.*

During the American Civil War in the 1860s, these insulting Valentines often attacked the political beliefs of the recipient. Interestingly, there do not appear to have been any vinegar Valentines aimed directly at people of non-European descent—likely because courting across color lines was practically unthinkable at that time.

In her diary, Helena Muffly of Pennsylvania wrote about her experiences sending and receiving such nasty Valentines. In 1911, she wrote about her relief at not having received any vinegar Valentines:

> *Tuesday, February 14, 1911: I guess that a good many people know that the fourteenth of February is St. Valentine's day. I expected at least one beautiful Valentine, but like some fools I was disappointed, but I didn't get any ugly ones either. I don't think I would have felt very much honored to be the recipient of one, but I was not the receiver of any. I, however, was the sender of four horrid ones. I sent some pretty ones, too.*

Helena sent nothing but vinegar Valentines the following year, showing just how common the custom had become:

> *Monday, February 12, 1912: Got my Valentines in preparation. They're all ugly ones. I thought one was most too much to send as it was rather mean looking. But I got it ready, so it has to go.*

DID YOU KNOW?

Some people collect Valentine's cards. There is even a group of collectors called the National Valentine Collectors Association.

Emily Dickinson's Comic Valentines

Awake ye muses nine, sing me a strain divine,
Unwind the solemn twine, and tie my Valentine!

–Emily Dickinson, "Awake Ye Muses Nine" (1850)

Not many well-known poets since the 17th century have left Valentine's poems among their corpus. The American poet Emily Dickinson (1830–1886) is one of the few who have.

Two Valentine's poems that Dickinson wrote to friends when she was young have survived. The first one, "Awake Ye Muses Nine," dates from Valentine's week 1850 and is the earliest known Dickinson poem. She wrote it for her father's law partner, Elbridge Bowdoin, and it is a comic Valentine of the type exchanged by friends.

Comic Valentines differed from the more common vinegar Valentines in being a form of good-natured fun rather than nasty criticisms. Comic Valentines might poke fun at the author or recipient, at some specific event or at an aspect of contemporary culture, such as the excessive romanticism of sentimental Valentines. Dickinson's Valentine's poem to Bowdoin mocked this romanticism as well as the fundamentalist religious zeal of many of those in her social circle, particularly at Mount Holyoke, the school she had attended.

"Awake Ye Muses Nine" mimics a Biblical sermon, with the first part expounding rather ridiculously on the notion of man and woman being made to join together as one, giving examples from throughout nature, and the second part is a more specific application of this exhortation to the recipient himself. The language of the first poem echoes the somewhat archaic language of the Bible, which is often found in the sentimental Valentines of the period.

For Valentine's Day 1852, Emily Dickinson sent a poem to William Howland, a tutor at Amherst College. "Sic transit gloria mundi" is a rather disjointed poem that was clearly written to someone with whom Dickinson had an ongoing conversation into which the poem fit. The poem parodies the political rhetoric of the time and mocks a variety of self-important character types. Interestingly, her father had just been elected to Congress.

Howland was so impressed with Dickinson's poem that he had it published in the *Springfield Republican* newspaper without her knowledge. Dickinson was reportedly so horrified when she saw it that she hid the newspaper from her father.

DID YOU KNOW?

Dickinson's first Valentine's poem says it was written during Valentine's week 1850. In the mid-19th century, it was customary to exchange Valentines over the course of a week because of the limitations of delivery and travel time.

Patriotic Valentines

When the Americans or the British were at war, card manufacturers produced Valentine's cards that reflected this state. This was true during the American Civil War (1861–1865), World War I (1914–1918) and World War II (1939–1945). The cards often depicted soldiers and sometimes Red Cross nurses. The verse or message might even reference the conflict, such as the following one on a Civil War–era card:

> 'Mid bugle's blast and cannon's roar,
> And 'mid the battles angry flame;
> 'Mid clashing sabres red with gore,
> I fondly breathe thy much-loved name.
> I feel thee near at dead of night,
> When I my vigil lone am keeping—
> Thy image guards me, angel bright,
> In dreams when wearied I am sleeping,
> Each northward wind wafts on its breath,
> To thee a yearning kiss of mine—
> On glory's field or bed of death,
> I live or die thy Valentine.

During World War I, the British government introduced rationing to aid the war effort, and people were issued ration cards for certain products. One card manufacturer came up with the idea to create a ration card for love. The card, given to many a sweetheart, claimed to have been issued by the Ministry of Love in Spooning Land. The holder of the card could use it to claim such items as a half-hour of kissing or an hour of squeezing.

Also during World War I, the Australian Imperial Forces issued some Valentine's cards that its soldiers could send to their wives or girlfriends back home. The verse on one of these cards stresses both the soldier's love for his sweetheart and his duty to his country:

> *Parting is hard, we must admit,*
> *The wrench requires some nerve,*
> *But you and I are both agreed*
> *The right thing is To Serve.*
> *Don't fear for me, remember this:*
> *To prove that I am true,*
> *No shot can strike me in the heart,*
> *For that I've left for you.*

 DID YOU KNOW?

British sailors onboard the HMS *Monmouth* posed in the shape of a heart for a Valentine's Day 2013 photo to send to their loved ones back home. The sailors were on their seventh tour of duty in the Persian Gulf.

Sender Unknown

Anonymous Valentine's cards have long been the custom in England, and prior to the 20th century, were common in Canada and the U.S., as well. Trying to guess the identity of the sender of the kind words was (and is) a large part of the holiday's fun.

In 1852, Peter Orlando Hutchinson of Devonshire expressed in diary entries his delight at the new custom of women sending Valentine's cards to men, but also his exasperation with not knowing the identity of the senders. On Valentine's Day, he wrote, "Received five Valentines! Sent thirteen!! Bless the girls! Why don't they put their names to them?" Then, on February 26, he added, "Three more Valentines! The lady in one of them asks me to kiss her! Why did she omit to put her name in some sly corner? In times past it has not been the custom for gentlemen to receive Valentines, but only to send them. The times, however, are changed: and the change came in last year—which was leap year. Now in Sidmouth at all events the gentlemen get as many as the ladies."

Anonymity enables people who are shy to partake in the fun and to feel more freedom to express their feelings. Shyness may have prompted the unknown sender of an 1842 Valentine's card to Laura Moorhead of Quebec City to write, "How shall my faithful heart my fair, declare the bliss it feels…"

The veil of anonymity also led to numerous incidents where the recipient wrongly guessed the sender's identity, leading to sometimes funny, sometimes embarrassing and occasionally tragic results. In *Cranford*, a television series based on Elizabeth Gaskell's novel of the same name, Caroline mistakenly believes that the Valentine's card she received, which referred to medicine, was sent to her by the town doctor. To compound the error, she further believes the Valentine is a proposal of marriage. In Thomas Hardy's 1874 novel *Far from the Madding Crowd*, Bathsheba Everdene sends an anonymous Valentine's card to an older, well-to-do bachelor living in her area, William Boldwood. The card, which reads "Marry Me," leads to Boldwood's obsession with the sender, whose identity he rightly guesses, and the series of tragic events that follows.

My fondest love,
These words express.
Dear Valentine,
The sender guess.
(from a mid-19th century English Valentine's card)

DID YOU  KNOW?

From 1938 to 1971, except for the war years, the Shell Motor Company sent anonymous Valentine's cards to its female clients.

Courting Cards

"My Katy Bee, my Katy Bee…keep your kisses all for me." Thus reads the Valentine from Catherine Worsley's chosen suitor, George Allanson Cayley. George put a lot of effort into this Valentine, writing the poem and painting the watercolor that surrounds it. He must have realized that Catherine had many suitors, as the watercolor depicts a woman being courted by several men. Clearly, he felt that a handmade card would be more favorably received than an expensive store-bought one, which he could no doubt have afforded.

George was correct in guessing that he was not Catherine's only suitor. Twenty-one other Valentines given to Catherine by ardent suitors can be found in the North Yorkshire County Records Office. They are a wonderful example of the important part Valentine's Day sometimes played in Victorian courtship.

The variety of Valentines reveals the variety of suitors for Catherine's hand. One man composed a letter in which he spoke of his accomplishments, like fighting in the Crimean War (1853–1856). Another man gave her a Valentine with scenes of domestic bliss. A third man told Catherine that despite his unattractive appearance, he was a good choice: "I'm ugly I know, but I'll presently show, that I really am not to be sneezed at." A fourth promised to do whatever it took to make her happy: "I'll gratify your slightest wish, whether t'were small or great, say the word at once you're heard, my pretty pretty Kate."

Catherine was considered a good catch, beautiful and from the lower nobility. Her father was Sir William Worsley of Hovingham, first baronet. The importance of her family name can be seen in a Valentine drawing in which her family's crest and that of her suitor are entwined. George Allanson Cayley, the man Catherine eventually married in 1859, was her cousin. It was common practice at the time to marry a close relation, thereby keeping a woman's dowry within the family.

His Whole World

Between 1844 and 1849, Frances Crocker, a woman from a well-to-do Worcester, Massachusetts, family, received dozens of Valentines from ardent suitors. One suitor acknowledged his competitors in his verse:

> *And I know that many love you,*
> *Many sue on bended knee;*
> *But whate'er you are to others,*
> *You're all the world to me.*

Valentine's Telegrams

♥ Canadian Pacific Railway offered Valentine's telegrams as early as 1912. Senders could choose from a variety of messages to be delivered in a pretty envelope.

♥ Some Valentine messages offered by Canadian Pacific Railway in 1912 were, "I picked my Valentine for life, sweetest and fairest of all, my wife," and " Faint heart, they say, ne'er won fair lady. My heart is strong for you this Valentine's Day."

♥ Valentine's telegrams were available in Great Britain between 1936 and 1982.

- ♥ Valentine's telegrams cost more than a regular telegram but were delivered on special holiday paper in golden envelopes.

- ♥ Artist Rex Whistler designed the first Valentine's Day telegram in Britain.

- ♥ In the year they were introduced in Britain, 50,000 Valentine's telegrams were sent.

- ♥ In Britain from 1942 to 1950, there was one all-purpose holiday telegram paper picturing a village scene with a couple at various life stages.

- ♥ In the U.S., Western Union was responsible for sending Valentine's Day telegrams.

- ♥ Western Union offered the sender a choice of ready-made telegrams or the option to compose one's own. It cost less to send a ready-made telegram.

- ♥ Some examples of Western Union's ready-made Valentine's greetings are, "Sign upon the dotted line. Say you'll be my Valentine," and "Too far to kiss you, but this greeting says I miss you, dear Valentine."

DID YOU KNOW?

In 1936, the British Post Office issued golden Valentine's telegrams for women wishing to propose because it was a leap year. Thousands of women sent out these special telegrams.

Valentines for the Times

It is often possible to judge the age of a Valentine's card based on what is pictured. Valentine's cards changed with the times and reflected current events, new technology, fashion trends and social attitudes. Some of the older Valentine's cards shock us with their blatant racism or even sexist violence. Others make you smile because what seemed innocent then is read as sexual innuendo now.

♥ In the 19th century, tomatoes were known as "love apples" and appeared on Valentines.

♥ In 1849, some companies produced California Valentines to commemorate the gold rush.

♥ During the early part of the 20th century, African Americans and Chinese Americans were frequently portrayed in a blatantly racist fashion on Valentine's cards.

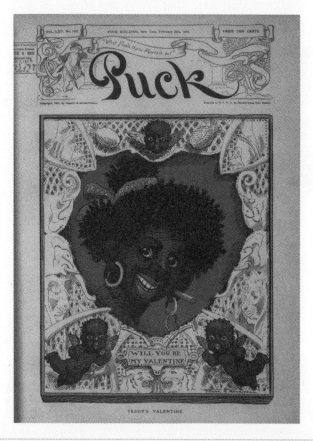

💜 Many Valentine's cards of the 1920s and 1930s were done in the art deco style popular at that time.

💜 During the Great Depression of the 1930s, when many men lost their jobs and took to the rails in the hopes of finding work, hobos were often shown on Valentine's cards.

💜 In the U.S., Valentine's cards commemorating the World's Fair held in New York in 1939–40 were printed.

💜 It is possible to date war Valentines by the uniforms worn by the soldiers depicted on the cards.

💜 The first Valentine's cards targeted at an African American middle-class appeared after World War II.

💜 Between the 1930s and 1950s, both going to the circus and exchanging Valentine's cards at school were popular with children. There are many circus-themed cards from this era.

💜 Some Valentines from the 1950s showed young people dancing to that new music craze, Rock 'n' Roll.

💜 During the 1950s and 1960s, the race to the moon was on and Valentine's cards depicting astronauts, rockets and other space-related objects were common.

💜 From the middle of the 20th century onward, Disney Valentine's cards featuring the studio's latest animated movie offerings have been popular with kids.

💜 Hit television shows or singing sensations are also featured on Valentines to cash in on their popularity.

💜 In the 1980s, Valentines with video game characters, such as the Mario Bros., first appeared.

💜 Goth Valentine's cards with dark humor are a product of the past two decades.

DID YOU KNOW?

The ribbons that adorn many Valentine's cards and are tied around boxes of chocolates were once symbols of love. A medieval lady would give her knight a token of her love when he competed in a tournament. This token was often a ribbon.

CUPID, FLOWERS AND CANDY: TRADITIONAL GIFTS AND SYMBOLS OF THE DAY

Creating Cupid

Come the beginning of February, everywhere you look you see hearts and pudgy, winged babies armed with a bow and arrows. A well-known symbol of Valentine's Day, Cupid is the son of Venus, the Roman goddess of love and beauty. Cupid's name translates as "desire." Over the centuries, he became interchangeable with the Greek god of love, Eros (son of Aphrodite).

Much about Cupid alludes to the unpredictable nature of love. Throughout the past, Cupid has been depicted as either a youth or an infant, both guises that allude to the often seemingly foolish and ridiculous nature of attraction. At times, Cupid is shown blindfolded to indicate that there is no way of knowing what will draw two people together. Cupid is winged because affections can be flighty and changeable.

CUPID, FLOWERS AND CANDY: TRADITIONAL
GIFTS AND SYMBOLS OF THE DAY

A Mini Messenger of Love

Scientists at Utah's Brigham Young University created a tiny
cupid for Valentine's Day 2013 using tiny nanotubes that measure only about 20 atoms in diameter. The finished product
was too small to be seen by the naked eye, but magnification
revealed the youthful god of love, complete with wings and his
trusty bow.

Cupid and Psyche: the Merging of Heart and Soul

An ancient Roman myth links the merging of heart and soul
to pleasure. In the myth, Cupid represents heart, his beloved
Psyche is soul, and their union as husband and wife results in
their daughter Voluptas—pleasure.

As the myth goes, Venus, the Roman goddess of love and
beauty, looked down from the heavens and frowned. Her temples were empty. Where were all the people that usually flocked
to them with offerings, hoping to gain success in love? She
noticed that many men were making their way to visit a young
woman of exceptional beauty rather than to her temples, and she
was furious.

Venus called on her son Cupid to take his bow and arrows along
with waters from the sweet and bitter fountains in her garden
and fly down to earth. There he was to seek out this woman,
whose name was Psyche, and, by striking her with one of his
arrows, cause her to fall in love with some horrible brute of
a man; Psyche would be punished, and men would go back to
bestowing upon Venus her due honor.

Cupid entered the bedroom of the sleeping Psyche. There he
dribbled some drops of the bitter water onto her lips to make
men admire her, but only from afar. Next, he touched her with
the tip of an arrow, which he then intended to shoot at some
poor, hideous-looking man, making the two fall madly in love.

But when the arrow touched the sleeping beauty, it woke her and she opened her eyes. Startled, Cupid accidentally cut himself with the arrow, and the god fell for the mortal woman. He fled back home in fear.

Meanwhile, though men continued to come to see the famed beauty, none came seeking her hand in marriage. Alarmed, her parents sought the advice of the priests, who informed them that their daughter's renowned looks had attracted the wrath of Venus. She would never marry a mortal man. Instead, her fate was to be wedded to a horrible monster who resided at the top of a mountain.

Psyche resigned herself to her fate. Standing on a rocky peak, she felt herself lifted up into the arms of Zephyr, the west wind, who carried her away to a meadow filled with flowers. Venturing over to a nearby grove of trees, she came upon a magnificent house filled with every luxury she could imagine.

A voice came out of nowhere and spoke to the girl, telling her that this palatial house was to be her new home. Everything she saw was hers and, even though she could not see them, she had many servants to fulfill her every wish. Her new husband would visit her there, but only at night under the cover of darkness.

He came to her that night and every night, and the two enjoyed many hours in each other's arms. However, Psyche longed to be able to see her husband's face, something he refused to allow.

As the days and nights passed, Psyche grew increasingly lonely. She begged her husband to allow the west wind to bring her two sisters to visit her. He agreed, and one day her sisters arrived at her door.

Seeing Psyche's wondrous home and then hearing about her mysterious but loving husband, the sisters were envious of

Psyche's good fortune. They encouraged Psyche to sneak a look at her husband while he slept.

Overcome by curiosity, Psyche decided to do just that. That night, after they had made love and her husband had fallen asleep, she lit a candle and held it close to his face. Expecting to see a hideous beast, she was so shocked to see the handsome face of a god that she accidentally dripped some wax onto him.

Awakened, Cupid was furious to discover that his wife had disobeyed him and now knew his identity. "True love," he told her, "is based on trust. You did not trust me even though I risked my mother's wrath to be with you. Now, I will leave you forever with nothing but your suspicions for company." Then Cupid and the mansion and all its servants disappeared.

Distraught, Psyche wandered the earth searching for her beloved. One day, she wandered into a temple of Ceres. The goddess of the harvest took pity on Psyche and told her that if she wanted to be reunited with her husband, she had to first appease the anger of Venus.

Psyche went to Venus' temple, where she begged her for mercy. Unmoved, the goddess demanded that Psyche complete three increasingly difficult tasks to prove her worth. With some divine help, Psyche was successful. Cupid, watching from above, was moved by his wife's devotion and went to Jupiter, the chief god, to beg for his help. Jupiter agreed to champion the lovers and was able to convince Venus to relent and allow her son to be united with the woman he loved. Psyche was brought to the heavens and given some of the gods' ambrosia to drink, making her immortal. Soon after, she gave birth to a daughter, who they named Voluptas. Thus, the merging to this husband and wife, of heart and soul, led to the creation of pleasure.

Feeling Lovey-dovey?

Doves are mentioned favorably in the Bible and were frequently used to symbolize the Holy Spirit. Doves also have a long association with love. The dove was a companion of many ancient goddesses of love and fertility, including the Greek goddess Aphrodite, the Syrian Atargatis, the Assyrian Astarte, the Sumerian Innana and the Akkadian Ishtar. According to Apuleius, a Roman writer from the 2nd century CE, doves pulled the carriage of Venus, the Roman goddess of love.

Doves mate for life, making them an ideal symbol for everlasting love. They are affectionate partners, providing support, companionship and sexual fidelity. Doves often will not choose a new partner if their first partner has died. The cooing noises that doves make sound to human ears like the tender words whispered by lovers.

Doves were highly thought of during the medieval period, when Valentine's Day likely originated. Medieval folk believed that doves, like many other birds, chose their mates on Valentine's Day. And because Geoffrey Chaucer mentioned doves in his Valentine's poem "The Parliament of Fowls," doves have been associated with Valentine's Day from its very beginning.

Oft have I heard both youths and virgins say,
Birds chuse their mates, and couple too, this day,
But by their flight I never can divine
When I shall couple with my Valentine.

–Robert Herrick, "To His Valentine, on
St. Valentine's Day" (1648)

Lovebirds

Lovebirds are a much more recent symbol of love sometimes seen on Valentine's Day. The term "lovebird" originated in the Middle Ages, along with the development of Valentine's Day as a celebration of love and a time for people and birds to choose their partners. "Lovebirds" is still a term used for lovers.

There is now a specific type of bird called a lovebird. These birds are small parrots. They received their name because, like doves, they mate for life and are known to spend long hours sitting cuddled together.

Now riseth the sun a pretty step to his fair height, and Saint Valentine calls the birds together, where Nature is pleased in the variety of love.

–Nicholas Breton, "Fantasticks" (1626)

Seeing Red

It seems as though everywhere you look on Valentine's Day, you see red—red hearts, red roses, red lingerie. The Muslim country of Saudi Arabia, which does not allow the celebration of Valentine's Day, bans the sale of all red items in the days leading up to February 14. Also, no one in the country is allowed to wear red clothes on that day. Why is the color red so closely associated with Valentine's Day and love?

It is easy to see why red is linked to hearts; it is the color of blood. And the heart is associated with love (and hence Valentine's Day) because prior to the modern era, the heart was considered the center of both the intellect and emotions.

The color red has been associated with sexuality since ancient times. It is linked to signs of arousal. It was the color of the ancient Greek phallic god, Priapus. When the Catholic Church established a system of linking colors with each of the seven deadly sins at the beginning of the 13th century, red was the color for the sin of lust. Even today, the areas in cities where prostitution occurs are known as red-light districts.

As Valentine's Day goes global, red is proving to be an appropriate color in other areas of the world, as well. In several Asian countries, such as China and India, red is the traditional color for brides to wear because it symbolizes good fortune. It is also the color of the sindoor dot worn by married Hindu women.

White and pink are the two other colors seen a lot around Valentine's Day. White generally symbolizes purity and fidelity, while pink is associated with warmth and affection.

DID YOU KNOW?

The ♥ as a symbol for love first appeared in French, German and Italian cities in the 14th century.

Say It with Flowers

Flowers are an excellent way to tell that special someone how you feel. Whether a single red rose or a bouquet of pink tulips, the gesture is almost always appreciated.

Roses are Red…

The connection between roses and love or passion goes back thousands of years, at least to ancient Greece. In the play *Medea* by Euripedes, Aphrodite, the goddess of sexual love, weaves wreaths of roses to wear in her long hair.

Several ancient Greek myths also associate Aphrodite (or her son Eros) with roses. In one, a new rosebush sprang from the earth at the very moment that Aphrodite arose from the foam of the ocean waves. The other deities spilled drops of nectar onto the plant; a rose instantly bloomed where each drop fell.

A better known myth involves the death of Adonis, one of Aphrodite's lovers. According to this story, Adonis is killed by a wild boar. Where drops of his blood fell on the ground, red roses grew up. In a different version of this tale, Aphrodite is racing toward her dying lover and steps on a thorn. Her bleeding foot dyes the white roses it falls upon red.

The ancient Romans also associated their goddess of love, Venus, with the sweet-smelling rose. In one Roman myth, roses sprang up from the ground wherever Venus walked. In another, her son Cupid was carrying a container of nectar to the gods on Mount Olympus when he tripped and spilled the nectar. Where the nectar seeped into the ground, red roses immediately started to grow.

So strong was the association between roses and the goddesses of sexual love in the ancient world that early Christians banned roses from churches. The connection between roses and sexual love endured nonetheless and expanded over time to include all types of love.

That roses have been such an enduring symbol of love has to do with the beauty of the flower as well as its sweet fragrance. Many people feel that the thorns are also apt because no love affair is without some painful experiences.

Not surprisingly, roses have long been linked to the declarations of love made on Valentine's Day. Valentines' poems mentioning red roses and blue violets date back to at least the 18th century.

Roses are red,
Violets are blue,
Sugar is sweet
And so are you.

Although the association of various types and colors of flowers with specific feelings dates back centuries, especially in the Middle East, it was the Victorians who most actively embraced the language of flowers. In a culture that frowned upon open displays of emotions, the Victorians had to find other ways to convey their true feelings. One method was through flowers. For example, if a woman in Victorian England wore a geranium, it meant she was depressed; a marigold meant grief stricken, and an anemone forsaken.

Roses in general conveyed feelings of love. However, the exact nature of these feelings depended upon the color of roses.

- ♥ Dark pink roses meant friendship and admiration.

- ♥ Pale pink roses conveyed grace, joy and happiness.

- ♥ Peach-colored roses signified modesty, gratitude, admiration and sympathy.

- ♥ Coral-colored roses meant desire.

- ♥ Orange roses signified fascination.

- ♥ Lavender-colored roses were a sign of enchantment and individuality.

- ♥ White roses symbolized purity and innocence.

❤ Red roses were a sign of passionate desire.

❤ A rosebud of any color stood for beauty, youth and an innocent heart.

❤ A red rosebud conveyed the message that the recipient was
very lovely.

Fewer people know the language of flowers today, but roses in
their many colored varieties still proclaim the same messages.
In France, these meanings are still widely understood and conveyed in gifts of bouquets on Valentine's Day. However, a French
woman is not likely to receive a dozen roses, but 11 or 13 because
odd numbers bring good luck.

DID YOU KNOW?

In February 2002, Thailand released rose-scented stamps showing a single red rose for Valentine's Day. In 2008, the Australian
commuter newspaper *mX* printed its Valentine's Day edition in
rose-scented ink.

Tulips Are Better than One

Tulips are the second most popular Valentine's Day flower
behind roses. In the Arabic world, tulips are the flower associated with love, passion and eternity. According to a Persian legend, a young man named Farhad fell in love with a woman
named Sharin. One day, he received a message that Sharin had
fallen ill and died. Beside himself with grief, Farhad jumped off
a cliff to his death in the hopes of joining his beloved in the
afterworld. The first tulips sprouted from the spot where his
body landed. Unfortunately for Farhad, Sharin was not in the
afterworld yet. A rival for Sharin's affections had sent him a false
report; Sharin was still very much alive.

In 2008, Turkey's Valentine's Day stamp had on it pink tulips, which symbolize caring and affection. To give red tulips to a woman is to declare one's love. If the flowers are variegated, it means the woman is thought to have beautiful eyes. Yellow tulips are emblematic of hopeless or unrequited love. The dark center of the flowers is said to represent the deep passion that a lover feels.

The Flowers of St. Valentine

It is not surprising that over the years several flowers have come to be connected with St. Valentine, as flowers have long been a favorite gift for many women to receive from their lovers. The violet is one flower associated with St. Valentine; the crocus is another. Violets, a sign of fidelity, are said to have grown outside St. Valentine's jail cell. According to one legend, St. Valentine used to take the blind girl in his care on long walks in the fields surrounding Rome, where she would pick bouquets of crocuses to give to her father. When St. Valentine was later in jail awaiting execution, he sent a final letter to the young girl, enclosing in its folds a pressed crocus. When the flower fell out, the girl's sight was miraculously restored. Every year since then, crocuses are said to bloom for the first time after the winter snows on the morning of February 14.

Another legend about St. Valentine says that an almond tree grew on the site of his grave, bursting into beautiful pink blossoms each spring as a sign of everlasting love.

DID YOU KNOW?

According to Gypsy folklore, if you see a crocus in bloom on Valentine's Day, you will be lucky in love for the next year.

Sweets for My Sweet

Every girl (and guy) likes to get something sweet from their sweetie on Valentine's Day. Chocolate is by far the most popular, but candy, in particular candy conversation hearts, also send the message of love.

Chocolate Delights

In 1861, Richard Cadbury came up with the idea of packaging chocolates in heart-shaped boxes for Valentine's Day. The idea was a huge success then and continues to be today, with 35 million heart-shaped boxes sold in 2013 alone! Since Cadbury's innovative boxes were first made, chocolate has been a favorite gift on Valentine's Day, and manufacturers are constantly looking for ways to make their chocolate or the packaging just a bit different and therefore more appealing to the consumer. Here are some of the more creative ideas that have appeared on store shelves in February:

❤ À la Mère de Famille in Paris offers chocolate padlocks for Valentine's Day. The specially made padlocks are decorated with a heart that looks like it has been scratched into the surface, as well as the couple's initials.

♥ Chocolats du CaliBressan offers an especially seductive chocolate gift for Valentine's Day—a pair of luscious-looking red lips! The treat inside is a double layer of milk or dark chocolate ganache and white chocolate surrounding tangerine liqueur.

♥ John & Kira's offers boxes of small, round, red, yellow and green chocolates decorated like ladybugs and bumblebees called "love bugs." Other companies also produce their own version of these amorous insects.

♥ Emily's Chocolates produces chocolate-covered fortune cookies that come packaged in red (love) and pink (friendship) take-out boxes for Valentine's Day. The fortune cookies contain messages of love and affection respectively.

♥ Small chocolate Miis with little red hearts on their chests are sold packaged in boxes resembling miniature Wiis—"Wii belong together, you and Mii."

♥ In Canada, special packages of red and pink Smarties are sold for Valentine's Day.

♥ In 2010, the Hakone Yunessun Spa Resort in Hakone, Japan, offered chocolate spas for Valentine's Day. Other spas in Japan and North America also offer various chocolate treatments to celebrate the Day of Love.

♥ Lovers can purchase edible chocolate paint for an evening of pleasure.

♥ Devine Foods of Rugby, Warwickshire, introduced chocolates with a kick for Valentine's Day 2013. Chili Chocolates are a spicy treat for those who enjoy candy with some zip.

DID YOU  KNOW?

In the U.S., February 14 is also National Creme-Filled Chocolates Day.

Getting Lucky with Chocolate?

Is chocolate an aphrodisiac? Many people, both past and present, believe it to be so, which no doubt plays into its popularity as a Valentine's Day gift. Chocolate definitely raises most people's spirits and is often eaten to give a person a little lift. Eating chocolate relieves stress and induces relaxation, which certainly makes it more likely that a person will become sexually aroused. Chocolate is known to contain phenylethylamine, which is the same chemical released by the brain during sexual intercourse or when one sees the object of their desire. It also contains serotonin, a known anti-depressant. So whether or not chocolate actually does increase a person's sex drive, giving chocolate as a gift on Valentine's Day is at least likely to make the recipient look upon you more favorably.

💜 The Aztec emperor Montezuma (d. 1520) reportedly drank 50 cups of chocolate each day to increase his sexual stamina. With 200 wives and concubines to satisfy, he probably needed all the help he could get!

💜 Early European explorers reported that the natives of Central America used to spread a chocolate paste on the body of their lover and nibble it off.

💜 When chocolate was prepared for England's Merry Monarch, Charles II (1630–1685), it was made with twice as many cocoa beans as normal. This was done to increase the king's sex drive, though from the number of mistresses he had, he was doing just fine without it!

💜 Louis Lémery, author of *Traité des ailments* ("A Treatise on Food," 1702), believed that chocolate was not only an aphrodisiac but also helped couples to conceive. (I suppose if you are having sex more often, you do increase the chances of conception.)

💜 The naturalist Carl Linnaeus (1707–1778) reported that chocolate was an aphrodisiac. He went on to name the tree that produces the cacao pods used to manufacturer chocolate *theobroma*, or "food of the gods."

💜 Jeanne, the Marquise de Pompadour (1721–1764) fed chocolate to her lover, King Louis XV (1710–1774), to increase his somewhat disappointing sex drive.

💜 Giacomo Casanova (1725–1798), the famous lover, believed that chocolate not only increased one's libido but also prevented one from catching syphilis. He regularly ate some chocolate before going out to seek another sexual conquest.

💜 In 1772, the notorious Marquis de Sade hosted a ball at Marseilles at which he provided his unsuspecting guests with confections made from two reputed aphrodisiacs, chocolate and Spanish fly. The result was a somewhat more bawdy ball than usual! The marquis was arrested soon after for his efforts.

DID YOU  **KNOW?**

Every February 14, Postmaster Stubbs of Romeo, Michigan, dresses in a tuxedo and delivers free chocolates along with Valentine's cards.

Candy Conversation Hearts

The idea of combining sweets with messages of love is not a new one. As far back as the 17th century, sweets made from sugar paste were cut into shapes, and messages written on pieces of paper were placed in the middle. Then, in 1866, sweets with short messages stamped on them with edible dye appeared. They were a hit!

♥ The New England Confectionary Company (NECCO) has been making candy conversation hearts since 1866. They sell 8 billion hearts annually.

♥ The heart shape of conversation candy only became standard in 1901. Prior to that year, a variety of shapes had been used.

♥ Candy conversation hearts were first produced in a factory in 1902.

♥ In Lucy Maud Montgomery's classic book *Anne of Green Gables* (1908), the feisty Anne crushes under her heel a candy heart with the motto "YOU ARE SWEET" given to her by Gilbert Blythe.

♥ Today, conversation candy is about relationships, but it was not always so. The temperance movement of the early 20th century adopted the idea and distributed candies with mottoes such as "Drink is the ruin of man."

♥ In Britain, Swizzels Matlow has produced candy conversation hearts since 1954, when they first appeared in holiday crackers.

♥ In the 1960s, Swizzels Matlow sold Golf Hints, a conversation candy with tips for golfers.

♥ In the U.S., candy conversation hearts are called Sweethearts. In Britain, they are called Love Hearts or Whatevers (exclusive to ASDA grocery stores).

♥ In the U.S., the candies are heart shaped. In Britain, the candies are round with the heart shape stamped onto the candy just like the mottoes.

♥ Every year, new phrases are introduced onto candy hearts. Also, some old phrases are abandoned (e.g., "DIG ME" and "YOU ARE GAY").

♥ In 2005, the new candy heart sayings revolved around a sports theme and included "#1 FAN" and "ALL-STAR."

💜 In 2007, animal-themed sayings were introduced, such as "LOVE BIRD," "TOP DOG," "PUPPY LOVE" and "BEAR HUG."

💜 The new 2009 phrases were food focussed: "SUGAR PIE," "HONEY BUN" and "SPICE IT UP."

💜 In 2010, consumers were able to participate in choosing the new phrases for the first time by taking part in an online survey. The results included the timely "TEXT ME" and "TWEET ME."

💜 In 2011, it was all about action: "SHAKE IT" and "U MOVE ME."

💜 In 2013, Swizzels Matlow produced One Direction Love Hearts. The packages contained hearts unique to each band member: "FOREVER ZAYN," "HOLD ME HARRY," "LOUIS LOVES ME," "ALWAYS NIALL" and "LIAM KISS ME."

💜 Despair, Inc. produces candy conversation hearts called Bittersweets for the broken-hearted. They have two varieties, one for the dumped and one for the dejected. Sayings include "FORGET WE MET," "JUST A FRIEND," "I MISS MY EX" and "WE HAD PLANS."

💜 NECCO also offers custom-made conversation hearts. You can make your own like Janice did in the first season of *Friends* when she gave Chandler a heart that read "Chan and Jan Forever."

💜 Trust Bart Simpson of *The Simpsons* to come up with conversation hearts with rude sayings as he did in the "I Love Lisa" episode (1993).

♥ Swizzels Matlow made special Love Hearts for Prince Charles and Lady Diana's wedding in 1981, and another special batch in 2011 when Prince William married Kate Middleton. Artist Mark Kennedy made a mosaic out of the hearts to celebrate the marriage of Will and Kate.

♥ In 2003, Swizzels Matlow made special Love Hearts to celebrate the 21st birthday of Prince William.

♥ Candy hearts are popular at engagement parties and weddings, not just on Valentine's Day.

♥ The "MARRY ME" hearts are among the most popular and are frequently used by men to propose.

♥ In 2003, British fashion designer Maya made a wedding dress entirely out of "MARRY ME" Love Hearts!

♥ In 2010, NECCO introduced new flavors of Sweethearts, including strawberry, apple, lemon, grape, orange and raspberry.

♥ Candy conversation hearts are also available in Spanish.

♥ Today, consumers can choose to buy sugar-free conversation hearts.

♥ People can skip the candy altogether and design their own virtual conversation heart online and email it to their sweetheart.

♥ Consumers can also purchase a variety of products, from cards to jewelry to kitchenware, with images of candy conversation hearts.

♥ The popular online game World of Warcraft features eight conversation hearts that players can exchange during the period around Valentine's Day.

♥ Candy conversation hearts are edible for five years.

♥ Candy conversation hearts are such a part of western culture that each year, the popular television game show *Jeopardy!* includes questions about them on its Valentine's Day episode. So memorize these bits of trivia in case you are ever a contestant on the show!

Beyond Chocolates and Roses

By far the most common Valentine's Day gifts worldwide are chocolates and roses, though other types of flowers and candy are also given. And, as at any time of the year, jewelry is always popular with the ladies. However, these standard gifts have not always been so standard.

A Dead Mouse for My Lady?

When cheap, manufactured Valentine's cards came on the market in the early part of the 19th century, the popularity of the holiday surged with all social classes in both England and the U.S. Throughout the century, merchants of almost every sort tried to find a way to cash in on the gift-giving craze (a practice that is still seen in stores and on the internet today). Probably the funniest attempt to capture this market is a newspaper ad from 1850: "The best Valentine yet—a box of Burgess & Co.'s Roach, Rat and Mouse Exterminator." After all, nothing says "I love you" like a box of poison and a bunch of dead rodents!

In the 21st century, consumers looking for something a little different can find almost anything with a heart pasted on it or made in a heart shape at this time of year. Red, pink and white packaging abounds. People can also purchase personalized gifts.

Love Trends

The trend in the U.S. is to purchase a gift for your pet on Valentine's Day. In China, tropical kissing fish are the latest fad, while in Portugal, gift baskets have long been the gift of choice. Kurdish couples present each other with clove-covered apples on Valentine's Day. The clove-covered apples (sometimes with the cloves in the shape of a heart) recall Adam and Eve and are symbolic of love and prosperity.

DID YOU KNOW?

Tasmanian farmer David Warren teamed up with engineer Josh Engwerda to grow the heart-shaped strawberries designed by Engwerda. The luscious berries are much in demand for Valentine's Day.

Celebrities' Valentine's Day Gifts Gone Wild

With their enormous incomes from acting, singing or playing sports, it should come as no surprise that celebrities tend to spend more on Valentine's Day presents than the average person. Some celebrities, however, have showered their special someone with truly extravagant gifts to celebrate their love.

♥ In 1969, actor Richard Burton gave his movie star wife Elizabeth Taylor a world-famous pearl for Valentine's Day. La Peregrina is one of the largest pearls in the world. It was discovered in the mid-16th century in the Gulf of Panama. It has been owned by English and Spanish royalty. Burton is known to have indulged his wife's love of jewelry. A year earlier, he had given her the 33.19-carat Krupp Diamond. Later in 1969, he purchased a 69.42-carat diamond that was named the Taylor-Burton Diamond. In 1972, for her 40th birthday, he bought her the historic heart-shaped Taj Mahal Diamond.

♥ A platinum cellphone worth $24,000 was rapper Jay-Z's Valentine's Day gift to his wife, singer Beyonce, in 2009.

♥ For Valentine's Day 2009, Bollywood actor Raj Kundra gave his wife, Shilpa Shetty, not only a gorgeous 48-carat heart-shaped diamond ring, but also a £5.5 million mansion in England!

♥ In 2010, Courtney Cox Arquette gave her then-husband, David Arquette, a funky Valentine's Day gift—an antique carousel horse worth about $45,000. The horse is hand-carved wood with a brass pole. Beautiful!

♥ Trust Angelina Jolie to come up with truly unique gifts for Brad Pitt. For Valentine's Day 2010, the actress got her man a 200-year-old olive tree to plant in the couple's olive grove at Chateau Miraval in France. In 2011, she bought him a waterfall for their home in California (!) as well as a diamond pendant (ho hum).

❤ As a Valentine's Day gift in 2011, singer Katy Perry bought actor Russell Brand a lilac-colored Bentley Brooklands valued at around $340,000. It was their one-and-only Valentine's Day together as husband and wife; the couple separated in December of that year and have since divorced.

❤ Singing sensation Justin Bieber bought out an entire floral boutique to surprise his girlfriend, singer Selena Gomez, for Valentine's Day 2011.

❤ For Valentine's Day 2013, soccer star David Beckham spent a fortune on his wife Victoria. The former Spice Girl received an $8 million Bulgari necklace. Wow!

❤ For Valentine's Day 2013, musician John Mayer gave Katy Perry a heart-shaped ruby ring worth about $5000. Not quite an $8 million Bulgari necklace, but still nice.

DID YOU  KNOW?

In 2013, consumer spending for Valentine's Day in the U.S. topped $18 billion!

LET'S CELEBRATE! VALENTINE'S DAY IN THE MODERN ERA

Locks of Love

In the past half-dozen years, couples have started to purchase padlocks, write their names on the locks, attach them to a landmark (often a bridge), and throw away the key as a symbolic and superstitious gesture that their love is eternal. It is believed that the practice began with its occurrence in the Italian novel *I Want You* by Federico Moccia, published in 2006. Not surprisingly, this new custom is especially popular around Valentine's Day, especially in Paris, the "City of Love," where couples attach personalized padlocks to a fence near the Pont des Arts Bridge and throw the keys into the Seine River.

Critics of the custom claim the locks are unsightly and that the keys thrown into rivers are just another form of pollution. Others worry that the additional weight of the locks will cause structural damage to the bridges. City governments have removed the padlocks from several bridges, including Toronto's Humber Bridge, Dublin's Ha'Penny Bridge, Seville's Puente

Isabel II, Brisbane's Kurilpa Bridge and Florence's Ponte Vecchio, for a variety of concerns ranging from aesthetic to structural.

❤ In Rome, couples affix padlocks to the Ponte Milvio, the same bridge mentioned in Moccia's inspirational novel.

❤ In Moscow, the current trend is for newlyweds to place a padlock on the Luzhkov Bridge.

❤ In Serbia, one bridge has acquired a new name because of the large number of padlocks attached to it—Most Ljubavi, or "Bridge of Love."

❤ A sign on Liverpool's Albert Docks reads, "This is a special place for lovers! Interlock your padlocks on the railings and throw away the key into the Mersey. You will never lose your true love!"

❤ On Valentine's Day 2010, the "Lock of Love" sculpture by the Dutch art collective BLISS opened in Rotterdam. It is a red loveseat made of steel fashioned in the shape of hearts to which couples can attach padlocks.

❤ A fountain in Montevideo, Uruguay, has a plaque inviting lovers to attach padlocks to it: "The legend of this young fountain tells us that if a lock with the initials of two people in love is placed in it, they will return together to the fountain and their love will be forever locked."

❤ In Taiwan, padlocks known as "wish locks" are placed at train stations to collect the energy from the passing trains.

❤ Master Lock created a website in 2012 where couples can purchase virtual padlocks to display in an online gallery.

Turning Valentine's Day Green

Consumers spend billions of dollars every year on cards, gifts and entertainment for Valentine's Day. Such a large amount of spending can hardly escape having an effect on both the environment and on the manufacturers of these products. Various organizations are raising concerns and are asking consumers to pay closer attention to the larger social and environmental impact of their purchasing choices.

Green Roses for Your Gal

Most of the roses that women in North America and Europe receive on Valentine's Day are grown in South America and Africa respectively. The flowers have to be flown to market and then driven to florists in climate-controlled vehicles. A 2007 study done by Cranfield University in England found that shipping 12,000 roses from Kenya to Britain for Valentine's Day bouquets resulted in 6000 kilograms of carbon dioxide emissions; the same number of roses grown in greenhouses in the Netherlands resulted in a whopping 35,000 kilograms of carbon dioxide emissions. However, many of the roses grown in Ecuador and bound for the U.S. for Valentine's Day are grown in a sustainable manner. Environmentally conscious consumers can look for bouquets labeled "organic" or "fair trade" or "sustainable."

A Sustainable Message of Love

Approximately one billion Valentine's cards are exchanged each year worldwide. That's a lot of paper and a lot of trees. The majority of these cards will end up in a wastebasket somewhere, which has environmentalists concerned. The Ian Somerhalder Foundation recommends three ways to send "green" Valentine's cards. First, you can make a card using recycled materials.

Second, you can make new plantable cards using old paper and seeds. Third, you can send an e-card.

In 2013, two elementary schools in Calgary, Alberta, took a big step and banned the exchange of Valentine's cards because of environmental concerns. Students were welcome to participate in other more environmentally friendly activities, such as wearing red and pink clothing. Ironically, the notice to parents and students about the ban was sent home on hundreds of sheets of paper.

Cheers to Love

Going out for a nice romantic dinner this Valentine's Day? Want to make the evening a bit different from your other date nights? Order one of the following wines or ales to go with your meal.

♥ Ladies, why not order a bottle of red or rosé Prince of Hearts wine to share with your very own Prince Charming? The label is appropriately decorated with a picture of Cupid.

♥ Looking for a bit of flirtatious fun this Valentine's Day? How about a bottle of Amberley Kiss and Tell moscato rosa wine?

♥ For the newlywed Valentine's couples, there is the California wine Monogamy: Truly, Madly, Deeply.

♥ Are you looking for love this Valentine's Day? There are wines for those with hopeful hearts, too. You can choose from Sexy, or promisQous, or that old stand-by, Boutielle Call (pronounced "booty call").

♥ Does your preference run more to beer than wine? Well, you can still find something (and someone?) to suit your taste this Valentine's Day! For the gals, there is Kilt Lifter Scottish-style ale by Four Peaks Brewing Company, while for the guys, Midnight Sun Brewing Company offers Panty Peeler beer!

♥ Or, chocolate is supposed to be an aphrodisiac, so why not try Sexual Chocolate Imperial Stout (9.5 percent)? The Foothills Brewing Company of North Carolina sells the beer for a short time before Valentine's Day each year.

Not Your Average Evening Out

If you're looking for something beyond dinner at a fancy restaurant, the following are some of the more "out there" ideas.

Having a Blast on Valentine's Day

For Valentine's Day 2012, Heartland Community College's Challenger Learning Center in Illinois offered couples the opportunity to take a simulated mission to the moon. Each couple's goal? To build and launch two sweetheart probes. Couples prepared for their mission with dinner and flowers.

Instructions were provided so they could complete their tasks. Afterward, a briefing was held to assess the success of their mission. Of course, such a unique evening out was bound to be a "far out" success!

A Flash Mob of Feathery Fun
It began as a flash mob in 2006 and has grown each year since then. Hundreds of people gather every year in San Francisco's Justin Herman Plaza to celebrate Valentine's Day with a huge pillow fight. Participants claim the unique festivities are a lot of fun and a great way to relieve stress. City officials are less impressed; the pillow fight results in a feathery mess that costs thousands of dollars to clean up.

Eternal Love
For all the zombie fans out there, Cutting Edge Haunted House in Dallas/Fort Worth, Texas, hosts a Valentine's Day Haunted House. Yes, you read that right. On February 14, the haunted house is populated with heartsick zombies clutching roses and chainsaws, searching for eternal love.

DID YOU KNOW?

The Original Philadelphia Ghost Tour Company offers a special Valentine's Day ghost tour called Love Never Dies.

Love Is in the Air
A charter company in Perth, Australia, offers couples the opportunity to become part of the Mile High Club on Valentine's Day. The twin-engine plane has a thick, heavy curtain separating the cockpit from the bedroom, where the couple spends an hour-long flight in each other's arms. After the flight, the couple receives a membership certificate and pin.

Love Stinks

You really have to wonder what your partner is trying to tell you if they take you to tour a sewage treatment facility on Valentine's Day. Do they think the relationship is crap, or just Valentine's Day? Regardless of the reasons, "urine" for a very smelly evening. Brooklyn's Newton Sewage Treatment Plant has been offering Valentine's Day tours since 2012. They are reputedly quite popular.

Aiming to Please

Are things a bit tense? Is your life full of stress? If you happen to be in England, take your significant other out to Frock Stock and Barrel Shooting School in Kent on Valentine's Day to learn to shoot clay pigeons and feel the tension melt away. Once you are feeling more at ease and relaxed, you can follow up with a romantic evening out.

Lovers' Leap

What better way to show your commitment to your relationship (or your need to be committed) than leaping off a bridge with your partner. Couples in England had the opportunity to try the Lovers' Leap tandem bungee jump on Valentine's Day 2013 in one of four cities—London, Manchester, Sheffield or Brighton. For couples lucky enough to survive this leap of faith, a half-bottle of champagne was provided afterward to celebrate and to calm the nerves.

DID YOU KNOW?

On Valentine's Day 1975, 120 British paratroopers returning from duty in Northern Ireland jumped, 16 at a time, into a field near Aldershot, Surrey, into the arms of waiting wives and sweethearts. It was billed as a St. Valentine's Day Lovers' Leap.

Sensual Satires
Many burlesque clubs in Britain offer special Valentine's Day performances. Go alone or take your partner. It is funny, entertaining and erotic all at the same time and can be a great mood-setter for your own private Valentine's Day festivities afterward!

Leather and Love
Prefer leather and love-knots to lacy lingerie? Then London's Torture Garden's Valentine's Dance is just the thing for you! This party is for fetishists of all kinds. Be sure to accessorize with studs and chains. No everyday clothing allowed.

Restaurant Romp
If you happen to be in Toronto on Valentine's Day, the Eatery, a restaurant in that city, allows customers to have sex in the washrooms on Valentine's Day! The door to each washroom has a lock, so sex cannot be considered public. Also, restaurants are considered private property in Canada, so the owners control what can and cannot occur on their premises.

Creative Ways to Say "I Love You"

Looking for a different or fun way to let that special someone know how you feel this Valentine's Day? Well, here are some suggestions:

♥ With sticky notes. For Valentine's Day, Claire Northcott of Paignton, Devonshire, covered her boyfriend Gordon Husband's pickup truck with 500 Post-it notes on which she had written, "I love you."

♥ With a poem. According to the *New York Knickerbocker* in 1845, the most oft-used rhymes for Valentine are divine, pine, shrine and mine.

♥ With a banner in the sky. Want the whole world to know how you feel about the man or woman you love? Tell them with a banner behind a plane.

♥ With a stamp. In 2003, Norway printed Valentine's Day stamps with a silver heart that could be scratched off to reveal one of several romantic greetings. For the more technologically savvy lovers, Taiwan offers Valentine's Day stamps featuring a Quick Response (QR) code printed within a perforated heart. Your lover can take a picture of the code with a cellphone to decode the message.

♥ With a newspaper ad. Valentine's messages began appearing in newspapers in Great Britain in 1975.

♥ With a cake or cupcake. Ice a cake or cupcake in red, white or pink frosting and write a few loving words on it. You can even buy a heart-shaped cake pan.

♥ With a chocolate heart. Melt of London makes hollow, lace-covered chocolate hearts for Valentine's Day. Hidden within the heart is a scroll that reads, "I Love You."

♥ With a message in a bottle. Decorate a bottle with hearts and ribbons this Valentine's Day. Write your sweetheart a love letter, roll it up and put it in the bottle.

♥ With a text message. British entrepreneurs Sam Seller and Oliver Levy operate a business that allows people to send anonymous Valentine's text messages. Senders pay by the line.

♥ With a billboard message. Lovebirds in Melbourne, Australia, can get their names displayed on Telstra's big Billboard of Love in the days leading up to Valentine's Day. Nothing says "I love you" more clearly than your name and your lover's name spelled out on a 26-meter LCD screen at one of the busiest intersections in Australia's second largest city.

DID YOU KNOW?

On Valentine's Day in colonial New York, women walked around with a knotted rope and hit every man they met with it.

Say It with a Postmark

Several towns and cities in the United States and around the world have very "Valentiney" names, and most do what they can to make the day extra special—and extra profitable. Although events vary from place to place, each town has one thing in common: it offers a special postmark for anyone who wants the Valentine they send to be marked by Cupid (so to speak).

America's Land of Love: Loveland, Colorado

♥ Loveland, Colorado, dubs itself the "Sweetheart City."

♥ The community was named after William A.H. Loveland, president of the Colorado Central Railroad.

💛 Beginning just after the end of World War II, the postmaster of Loveland began receiving requests for Valentine's cards to be postmarked from the "land of love." The town requested and received permission to use a special Valentine's Day postmark.

💛 Over 300,000 Valentine's cards arrive in Loveland every year to be stamped with the special postmark. The task of stamping all these envelopes has fallen to a group of senior citizens who volunteer their services each year.

💛 Since 1962, the town has selected a Miss Loveland Valentine.

💛 Every year since 1964, the Loveland Chamber of Commerce holds a contest for the best Valentine design and verse. The winning selection is made into a special Valentine's Day card and mailed to people throughout the world who have requested one.

💛 The Thompson Valley Rotary Club is responsible for Loveland's Valentine Hearts Program. Large wooden red hearts are attached to light posts throughout the community. People can pay a fee to have their personal message of love painted in white on a heart for all to read.

💛 The Loveland Ski Area has been holding an annual Valentine's Day wedding event for the past 22 years. It is called Marry Me & Ski Free. Couples get married or renew their marriage vows on the mountaintop and can then enjoy the rest of their special day skiing together.

💛 Bleeding Hearts is the name of a porter brewed with cherries and cocoa nibs by Grimm Brothers Brewhouse, a local microbrewery.

DID YOU KNOW?

Colorado also has a town called Romeo.

American Valentines

Valentine, Nebraska

- ♥ Valentine, Nebraska, calls itself "Heart City."

- ♥ The community was named for an early resident, Edward Kimball Valentine.

- ♥ Since the 1930s, a local King and Queen of Hearts has been elected at the local high school.

- ♥ Restaurants in Valentine serve heart-shaped steaks on Valentine's Day.

- ♥ A huge red heart is painted on Main Street. Smaller hearts adorn the sidewalk.

- ♥ The street signs in the town are red, with the direction placed within a heart.

- ♥ Every year, the local post office affixes a special holiday postmark on hundreds of Valentines.

Valentine, Texas

- ♥ The town of Valentine, Texas, is known as the "Love Station of Texas."

- ♥ The town got its name because the first train to arrive in the town did so on February 14.

- ♥ Since 1983, the village has offered special love postmarks for Valentine's Day greetings. Twenty years later, they were receiving 19,000 cards to postmark. The community of Valentine, Texas, has fewer than 200 inhabitants.

♥ The town's holiday postmark changes every year and is the winning design of entries from the local grade 7 to grade 12 students. The 2008 design featured two teddy bears holding hearts.

DID YOU  KNOW?

Abolitionist and former slave Frederick Douglas (d. 1895) did not know which day he was born on. He chose to celebrate his birthday on February 14 because his mother used to call him her Valentine when he was a child.

More of Cupid's Towns

♥ Mail your Valentine's card early this year to Loveville, Maryland, where the postmaster will put a special postmark on it and send it on its way to your beloved.

♥ Romance, Arkansas, offers people the opportunity to re-mail their love letters or wedding invitations with a special romantic postmark. In 2004, the postmark was a dove with a ribbon stating "Love is in the Air" trailing from its beak. The 2005 postmark featured Cupid with his bow and arrow. In 2009, the postmark was a winged heart with the motto "From My Heart to Yours."

♥ Romeo, Michigan, and Juliette, Georgia, have teamed up since 1994 to provide a joint postmark for Valentine's Day.

♥ Love, Saskatchewan, was the first post office in Canada to offer a special Valentine's Day postmark in 1984. The postmark that year featured a teddy bear holding a heart. Postmistress Pauline McKinnon and her husband came up with the idea. It took them five years to get permission from Canada Post to use the postmark; it was the first time the government had allowed a community to have its own unique postmark.

♥ Saint-Valentin, Quebec, began offering a special postmark on its name day in 1994.

♥ Since then, two more Canadian communities have received their own unique Valentine's Day postmarks—Cupids and Heart's Content, both in Newfoundland. Newfoundland and Labrador is clearly Canada's love province; besides Cupids and Heart's Content, it also boasts Heart's Delight, Heart's Desire, L-Anse-Amour and Little Heart's Ease, not to mention Conception Bay!

❤ The French village of Saint-Valentine in Indre holds a number of tourist events on February 14, including marriage vow renewals. It bills itself as the "Village of Love" and has even planted a garden of love. Since 1967, the post office there has used special postmarks for Valentine cards and letters. From 1967 to 1979, the postmark was two entwined hearts designed by Jean-Louis Boncoeur. From 1980 to 1984, it was a flame of love by Raymond Peynet.

❤ The English hamlet of Lover in Wiltshire once had a special Valentine's Day postmark, but the post office was shut down in 2008. The 2002 postmark featured a box of chocolates and a rose surrounded by hearts.

Zoo You Love Me?

Certain birds have been linked with Valentine's Day from its very beginning. Recently, other animals have been included as well. Not wanting to miss out on a major money-making occasion, zoos around the world have come up with creative ways of drawing crowds of lovers on Valentine's Day.

❤ For Valentine's Day 2013 in New York City, the Bronx Zoo came up with a very strange way to show your love. For $10, you could name a Madagascar hissing cockroach after your loved one! The money was used to fund wildlife conservation projects in the African nation.

❤ San Francisco Zoo is just one of many zoos that offers adult couples the opportunity to learn about and observe the mating habits of various animals on Valentine's Day.

❤ Officials at Yunnan Wild Animal Park in China held a cross-species wedding ceremony between Changmao, a ram, and Chunzi, a doe, on Valentine's Day 2012.

♥ Silver and Zorka, two Shetland ponies, were united in a mock wedding ceremony at the Royev Ruchey Zoo in Krasnoyarsk, Russia, on Valentine's Day 2013. The equine couple was dressed in a tux and wedding gown.

♥ Kathryn O'Connor and James Oliver exchanged marriage vows underwater at the London Aquarium on Valentine's Day 2010, surrounded by fish and giant sea turtles.

♥ The animals at Seattle's Woodland Park Zoo were not left out of the Valentine's Day festivities in 2010. Zoo staff prepared special treats for them, such as heart-shaped steaks and heart-shaped fruit juice ice pops.

♥ Jaguars at California's San Diego Zoo were fed heart-shaped treats made from beef blood and pieces of meat for Valentine's Day 2013.

♥ Also in 2013, visitors to the California Academy of Science were given the opportunity to write Valentine's Day messages on large red paper hearts for the academy's resident penguins.

Q: What did the boy owl say to the girl owl on Valentine's Day?

A: Owl be yours!

Q: What did the boy squirrel say to the girl squirrel on Valentine's Day?

A: I'm nuts about you!

Valentine's Day Proposal Packages

A few retailers have tried to profit from the love and romance in the air in mid-February by offering men unique ways to propose on Valentine's Day. In 2012, Pizza Hut offered men a $10,000 Valentine's Day engagement package: pizza, breadsticks, flowers, fireworks and a ruby engagement ring delivered in a limo and accompanied by a professional photographer to capture the special moment.

Also that year, Cupcakes Gourmet in Philadelphia offered a special for guys looking for a way to propose on Valentine's Day. For $55,000, a man could purchase a red velvet cupcake with an 8-carat diamond engagement ring as a decoration!

Diamonds Are Forever

Diamonds were just one of many gemstones used in engagement rings prior to the 20th century; they were no more popular than any other type of gemstone. That changed when De Beers needed to find a way to sell the huge piles of diamonds it was mining in South Africa. De Beers solved their problem in an ingenious way: they created an artificial but very strong connection in people's minds between diamonds, something they do not need, and love, something they both need and want.

This linking of diamonds and love was secured by the most powerful marketing slogan in history: "A diamond is forever." It was Frances Gerety, a copywriter at the New York advertising firm N.W. Ayer, who came up with the slogan in 1947. Since then, it has become a source of male pride to give a woman a diamond engagement ring. Indeed, it is almost expected.

Millions of men worldwide choose February 14, Valentine's Day, as the day to pop the question. Since 1998, human rights' organizations have been encouraging men to buy their sweetheart a diamond that is conflict-free. According to the United Nations, conflict diamonds "originate from areas controlled by forces or factions opposed to legitimate or internationally recognized governments, and are used to fund military action in opposition to those governments, or in contravention of the decisions of the Security Council." In other words, these diamonds (also known as "war diamonds" or "blood diamonds") fund armed conflicts (e.g., in Sierra Leone, Angola and Liberia). In Africa, where most of these types of diamonds originate, diamonds have gone from being the means to fund a rebellion to being the reason for the revolt itself.

In 2001, the World Diamond Council was formed in Belgium. Its purpose is to speak on behalf of the industry in matters involving blood diamonds. The council also created the Kimberley Process, an international agreement to try to prevent trafficking in blood diamonds. The 75 members of the council are only allowed to trade rough diamonds with other members. All diamonds are supposed to be accompanied by a certificate listing their country of origin. However, the Kimberley Process has proven to be largely ineffective because it relies on the voluntary participation and honesty of all participants. There is no standard certificate of origin for diamonds and no other reliable method for establishing the origin of a diamond, so the process is based upon the hope that smugglers and revolutionaries will be honest! No wonder it rarely works.

Nevertheless, men purchasing a diamond for their sweetheart this Valentine's Day are encouraged to do their best to ensure that it is as conflict-free as they want their relationship to be.

Celebrity Love on Valentine's Day

Valentine's Day Engagements

♥ Porno for Pyros bassist Martyn LeNoble chose Valentine's Day 2010 to propose to his girlfriend, actress Christina Applegate. The couple kept their engagement a secret for two months.

♥ British entrepreneur, television personality and lifelong bachelor Simon Cowell finally proposed at the age of 50 to girlfriend Mezghan Hussainy on Valentine's Day 2010. He later said the engagement was a mistake, and the couple split.

♥ Actor Harrison Ford proposed to his long-time girlfriend, actress Calista Flockhart, on Valentine's Day 2009. The couple started dating in 2002, and despite a 22-year age difference, are still together.

♥ Controversial radio star Howard Stern proposed to Beth Ostrosky on Valentine's Day 2007 with a 5.2-carat, emerald-cut diamond engagement ring valued at a quarter of a million dollars, which Stern himself had designed.

♥ Emraan Hashmi, a Bollywood actor known as "the serial kisser" for his Casanova-like roles, dated Parveen Shahani for six-and-a-half years before proposing on Valentine's Day 2006. Hashmi recalls their engagement as the most romantic moment of his life.

💜 Singer Christina Aguilera received a 5-carat diamond and platinum engagement ring from boyfriend Jordan Bratman on Valentine's Day 2005. The couple divorced in 2010.

💜 Bollywood actor and dancer Hrithik Roshan got down on one knee in the sand at Juhu Beach in Mumbai and proposed to his girlfriend Suzanne Khan, a fashion designer, on Valentine's Day 2000.

Valentine's Day Weddings

💜 2013: celebrity wedding designer Preston Bailey and Theo Bleckmann

💜 2012: actress Monique Coleman and Walter Jordan

💜 2011: actress/model Natasha Henstridge and singer Darius Campbell

💜 2009: supermodel Adriana Lima and basketball player Marko Jaric; actress Salma Hayek and businessman François-Henri Pinault

💜 2008: musician Liam Gallagher and Nicole Appleton

💜 2007: actress Keri Russell and Shane Deary; singer Blaze Bayley and Debbie Hartland

💜 2004: actress Rosa Blasi and New York Giants fullback Jim Finn

💜 1999: actress Diane Ladd and Robert Charles Hunter; Bollywood actress Mandira Bedi and movie director Raj Kaushal

💜 1998: actress Sharon Stone and *San Francisco Chronicle* editor Phil Bronstein; Bollywood actor Sanjay Dutt and Rhea Pillai

♥ 1996: singer Prince and his back-up singer Mayte Garcia; Bollywood actor Arshad Warsi and MTV VJ Maria Goretti

♥ 1995: actress Roseanne Barr and her bodyguard Ben Thomas

♥ 1994: guitarist Jerry Garcia and Deborah Koons

♥ 1991: actress Meg Ryan and actor Dennis Quaid; talk show host Leeza Gibbons and actor/architect Stephen Meadows

♥ 1984: musician Elton John and Renate Blauel, a recording engineer

♥ 1974: singing duo Daryl "The Captain" Dragon and Toni Tenille

♥ 1958: actress Rita Hayworth and movie producer James Hill

♥ 1613: Princess Elizabeth Stuart of England and Scotland and Frederick V, Elector Palatine. On the occasion of their marriage, the poet John Donne wrote the following poem:

> *Hail, Bishop Valentine! whose day this is;*
> *All the air is thy diocese,*
> *And all the chirping choristers*
> *And other birds are thy parishioners:*
> *Thou marryest every year*
> *The lyric lark and the grave whispering dove;*
> *The sparrow that neglects his life for love,*
> *The household bird with the red stomach;*
> *Thou mark'st the blackbird speed as soon,*
> *As doth the goldfinch or the halcyon…*
> *This day more cheerfully than ever shine*
> *This day which might inflame thyself,*
> *old Valentine!*

DID YOU  KNOW?

Salma Hayek and François-Henri Pinault, who married on Valentine's Day 2009, named their daughter Valentina.

Strange Valentine's Day Weddings

Not for the Faint of Heart
Boonthawee Seangwong and Kanjana Kaetkeow were married in Thailand on Valentine's Day 2006. The couple were painted deathly pale with fake blood and scars. There were live centipedes and scorpions. The bridal suite was even shaped like a coffin!

I Choco-do!
Sitting in a bathtub full of cooled liquid chocolate in a New York City restaurant, chocoholics Melanie Lugo and Kevin Kuhlman exchanged wedding vows. The wedding took place on February 14, 1997.

Odd Couples
On Valentine's Day 2001, a double wedding ceremony was held in Ayuthaya, Thailand. The couples being wed were two pairs of elephants! The elephants were dressed smartly (or ridiculously) for the occasion in red-hearted gowns. Their trunks were painted in bright colors.

Shotgun Weddings
On February 14, 2013, Guns and Ammo Garage in Las Vegas offered a unique free wedding ceremony or vow renewal for gun fanatics. The ceremony took place in front of a photo of a land-scape strewn with guns, as well as a photo of an arch made of

guns. The ceremony was officiated by the Pistol Packing Preacher, the Reverend Jimmy McNamara. Following the ceremony, the couples were allowed to use the shooting range for free.

Love Is Blind

Love must truly be blind, for how else do you explain the wedding of Edith Casas (23) and Victor Cingolani (28) on Valentine's Day 2013 in Argentina? Cingolani is the former boyfriend and convicted murderer of Edith's identical twin sister Johana. Cingolani says he is innocent, and Edith says she believes him. Her mother tried to get the courts to ban the marriage but was unable to do so. Her father says she is dead to him. Cingolani is serving a 13-year sentence.

DID YOU  KNOW?

Valentine's Day and New Year's Eve are the two busiest days for Las Vegas wedding chapels.

Valentine's Day Promotions

Like it or not, Valentine's Day is a largely commercially driven holiday. The following business promotions attest to this fact.

Marmite You Be My Valentine?

Marmite, a spread made from yeast, salt and vegetable extracts, is popular in Britain and Australia (if nowhere else). For Valentine's Day 2008, Lover's Marmite, with the additional ingredient of champagne, was introduced to the market. Fifty jars with silver engraved lids were also offered for sale.

That same year, in honor of Valentine's Day, Guernsey sculptor Jeremy Fattorini made a replica of Rodin's famous sculpture "The Kiss" from 420 jars of the champagne Marmite. The sculpture, which took the artist two and a half weeks to create, was put on display in Greenwich Park in London.

In 2013, the producers of Marmite put together an aggressive advertising campaign to capture the Valentine's Day consumers. The ads (five in all) each targeted a specific type of bad date and encouraged people to forego the awful Valentine's dates and go for a sure thing instead. What's that? You guessed it! Marmite. The five types of bad dates featured in the ads were the Night Hunter (a sexually aggressive older woman), the Clingon (the obsessed stalker type), the Wolf Whistler (the guy who is a player), the Life Sucker (the negative or fun-killing person) and the Beefcake (all looks and no substance).

DID YOU KNOW?

For Valentine's Day 2013, London's Madame Tussaud's allowed people to take their picture with the wax figure of actor George Clooney sitting on a park bench.

A Gown of Roses

British supermarket giant ASDA wanted a unique way of promoting the sale of flowers for Valentine's Day 2012. The result was a stunning gown made from 1725 red flowers, including roses, chrysanthemums, gerberas and carnations. The form-fitting dress was designed by florist Joe Massie. To complete the ensemble, the model wore stilettos covered in red rose petals.

DID YOU KNOW?

A portrait of the Duke and Duchess of Cambridge was made entirely of flowers by Joseph Massie in Trafalgar Square, London, for Valentine's Day 2013.

Valentine's Day Baby?

In February 2013, IKEA offered a special Valentine's Day promotion at their Australian stores. In their flyer was a coupon for a free crib for babies born on November 14, 2013 (nine months after Valentine's Day). Wonder how many Aussies will be claiming their free cribs come November?

Kiss for a Cause

Procter & Gamble, the maker of Puffs Facial Tissues, ran a Valentine's publicity and charity event from February 1 to 24, 2013. People logged on to the Puffs Facebook page and selected a kiss that looked like an imprint left on a tissue after blotting lipstick. There were 50 kisses in various categories, such as Flirty, and in different colors. Each one came with a loving message attached. For every kiss shared on Facebook, the company donated $1 to Dress for Success, a charity that helps disadvantaged women to achieve economic independence.

Pucker Up!

Not surprisingly, Valentine's Day sees a lot of kissing. Some couples, however, have taken it to the extreme.

💜 On Valentine's Day 1999, 3000 couples in the eastern European country of Belarus participated in a simultaneous kiss.

💜 Nontawat Jaroegenasornsin (31) and Thanakorn Sittiamthong (28) kissed for 50 hours and 25 minutes to become the *Guinness Book of World Records* winners for the longest kiss. Couples had to remain "kissing" while eating, drinking and even using the toilet. Along with the record, the winning couple received a night in a 5-star hotel, $6500 in diamond rings and some cash.

💜 For Valentine's Day 2012, a restaurant in Shanghai, China, gave a free meal to couples who participated in a one-minute kissing contest.

💜 The world's largest group kiss occurred in Mexico City on February 14, 2010: 39,897 people participated.

💜 On Valentine's Day 2012, Chris Kay Fraser of Toronto, Ontario, launched Canada's Kiss Map, an online forum where people can share stories of especially memorable smooches. Around 700 stories were posted on the first day!

DID YOU KNOW?

There is a town in Germany named Kissing.

Valentine's Day Love Songs

Here are some real Valentine's Day love songs to add to your playlist for that romantic evening with your honey.

💜 For opera enthusiasts, there is Georges Bizet's *La Jolie Fille de Perth* (1867), based on Sir Walter Scott's novel *The Fair Maid of Perth: Saint Valentine's Day* (1828). It is a story of several suitors who contend for the hand and heart of Catherine, the fair maid of Perth. The story begins on the eve of St. Valentine's Day.

💜 "My Funny Valentine" (1937) is a show tune written by Lorenz Hart (lyrics) and Rodger Richards (music) for the musical *Babes in Arms*. The singer pokes fun at her sweetheart but then says that she loves him just the way he is. The song has been recorded by over 600 artists, including Ella Fitzgerald and Barbra Streisand.

💜 Bruce Springsteen wrote a song called "Valentine's Day" in which a man asks a woman to be his Valentine, saying that the only thing that scares him is a life without her. It was released in 1987.

💜 In Steve Earle's 1996 "Valentine's Day," the singer regrets forgetting to buy his sweetheart any gift for Valentine's Day, saying all he has to offer her is his love, which he hopes is enough. The song was used in the 2006 movie *Talladega Nights*.

💜 In 1997, American country singer Martina McBride recorded "Valentine" by Jim Brickman. The song tells of a love that will last forever.

💜 In 2008, Nigerian R&B singer Faze released the song "Valentine's Day." It quickly became a hit in Africa. The song is about being sure to show the one you love how much you care for them on Valentine's Day.

💜 Kina Grannis won Sirius Radio's Coffee House Singer/ Songwriter Discovery of 2010 with her single "Valentine." In this song, Grannis sings that she loves her man every day as he loves her and that, while they don't need a special day to express their love for each other, there is no reason not to take advantage of the opportunity to do so on Valentine's Day.

💜 Paul McCartney wrote and recorded a song called "My Valentine" in 2011. In it, he sings about his undying love for a woman.

DID YOU KNOW?

Singer Janis Ian received 461 Valentine's Day cards in 1977 after confessing in her song "At Seventeen" that she had never received one!

LET ME CALL YOU SWEETHEART: VALENTINE'S DAY LOVE STORIES

A Sweet Heart Indeed!

Ever wonder where the term "sweetheart" originated? To the find the answer, we need to delve 750 years into the past.

Lady Dervorgilla loved her husband, John de Balliol. The couple had not known each other when their families arranged a marriage between them 35 years earlier to increase each family's wealth and power. In the intervening years, love grew and 12 children were born to them—six boys and six girls (their eldest son, John Balliol, would become king of Scotland in 1292). The couple were major landowners in Scotland and England, and John was a political advisor to the English king Henry III.

The couple founded Balliol College at Oxford as well as several religious institutions.

When John died in 1268, his wife was devastated. As was the custom among the aristocracy at the time, Dervorgilla had her husband's heart removed from his body and embalmed. Contrary to popular tradition, she did not bury his heart in a separate location; she had the organ placed in an ivory casket and kept it with her at all times. She referred to it as her "sweet, silent companion."

In 1273, Lady Dervorgilla founded yet another religious institution, an abbey in the county of Galloway in Scotland. This abbey, the last Cistercian monastery to be built in Scotland, was founded in memory of Dervorgilla's late husband. When Lady Dervorgilla died in 1289, she was buried in the monastery's church; in her hands was placed the ivory box holding her late husband's heart. To honor the loving devotion of their founder, the monks began to call the abbey *Dulce Cor*, or "Sweet Heart." By the 15th century, "sweetheart" had become a term of endearment.

The practice of a separate burial for hearts and bodies continued among Scotland's upper classes into the 17th century. The practice occurred in other parts of Europe, as well. It continued a century longer in France, Scotland's long-time ally.

DID YOU KNOW?

In 2013, Farmville created the Sweetheart Tree for Valentine's Day. Players can build their own Sweetheart Tree and craft Valentines to exchange with other players.

Her Valentine by Choice

In the 17th century, most marriages among members of the English upper classes were made to create family alliances or to gain a fortune or title. The marriage between Sir William Temple (1628–1699), first baronet, and Dorothy Osborne (1627–1695) was different; the couple married for love. William and Dorothy met and fell in love in 1647. Their fathers disapproved of the match and refused to allow the couple to marry. Dorothy's parents put a great deal of pressure on her to marry a suitor of their choice, but she steadfastly refused, even when presented with the opportunity to marry the son of Oliver Cromwell, Lord Protector of England. William and Dorothy were finally able to wed in 1655, following the deaths of both their fathers.

During the intervening years, William and Dorothy had carried on a secret courtship by writing letters to each other. Many of Dorothy's letters from this period survive. One of them describes how she spent Valentine's Day 1654/5:

> *I'll tell you something that you don't know, which is, that I am your Valentine and you are mine. I did not think of drawing any, but Mrs. Goldsmith and Jane would need make me write some for them and myself; so I writ down our three names, and for the men, Mr. Fish, James B., and you. I cut them all equal and made them up myself before they saw them, and because I would owe it wholly to my good fortune, if I were pleased, I made both them choose first that had never seen what was in them, and they left me you. Then I made them choose again for theirs, and my name was left. You cannot imagine how I was delighted with this little accident…. I was not half so pleased with my encounter next morning. I was up*

*early, but with no design of getting another Valentine
and going out to walk in my night-clothes and night-
gown, I met Mr. Fish going hunting, I think he was;
but he stayed to tell me I was his Valentine.*

Dorothy teased William that she would have considered taking
Mr. Fish for her Valentine if he had bothered to powder his hair!

William was definitely Dorothy's Valentine by choice, as she was
his. The couple were married for 40 years until Dorothy's death
in 1695. They had nine children, all of whom they outlived.

*Choose me your Valentine,
Next let us marry.*

–Robert Herrick, "To His Mistress" (1648)

Love and War

Thinking of You

When Robert King of Virginia joined the Confederate Army, he
left behind his beloved wife Louiza. Robert missed his wife and
thought of her a great deal, as shown by some of the handmade
gifts he sent her, including a clever Valentine's card. Robert took
a piece of pink paper from an advertisement as well as a white
envelope, folded each and cut them into strips. These he wove
together to form a heart with seemingly random holes. When the
heart was unfolded, the purpose for the holes was made clear.
The heart unfolded to reveal two rather crude figures, a man and
a woman, sitting on a bench crying. Sadly, Robert never saw
Louiza again. He was killed in the war.

A Great Love from the Great War

A year before the outbreak of World War I, young Edith Dunn of Derbyshire met the man of her dreams. Will was a soldier serving in the same regiment as Edith's brother Tom. In 1914, the war started, and Will and Tom were shipped over to France to fight. Neither man survived. Edith was crushed. She never recovered from the loss of her love Will, and she never married, though she lived a long life. When she died in 1970, two Valentine's cards were found among her possessions. They were the ones she had received from Will way back in 1913 and 1914. She had treasured them as she had treasured him for the rest of her life.

Valentines for Veterans

The Korean War (1950–1953) is sometimes referred to as the "Forgotten War." However, Canadian veterans of the war who were long-term patients at the Perley and Rideau Veterans Health Centre in Ottawa were pleased to discover on Valentine's Day 2010 that some people still remembered their efforts to keep South Korea free from Communism. The veterans received handwritten Valentine's cards from students at Yongsin High School in Pohang, South Korea. The students were learning English from Michelle Rehberg, a Canadian who taught them about the part Canada played in the Korean War as a member of the United Nations.

More Valentine's Day Love Stories

Undying Love

John and Sue Johnston of Houston, Texas, had been married for 46 years when John passed away in 2011. The following Valentine's Day, Sue received a beautiful bouquet of flowers from John just as she had every year for 46 years. When she inquired at the florist's about the delivery, she was told that before he died, her husband had prepaid for that delivery as well as deliveries for many years to come! According to Sue, when John was alive, the note attached to the Valentine's Day bouquet always read, "My love for you grows." Now, the note reads, "My love for you is eternal."

Two Hearts Entwined

British couple Doris and Harry Ward have celebrated Valentine's Day with the same card for over 70 years. Harry gave the card to his girlfriend Doris before leaving for war on February 14, 1941. Every year since then, Doris has displayed the card on the couple's mantelpiece on Valentine's Day. The card reads, "Two hearts entwine this Valentine. True love makes it sincere." The couple married in 1942 and have two daughters, two granddaughters and four great-grandchildren. Harry has never had to buy Doris another Valentine's card.

Secret Admirer

In 1928, 16-year-old Meryl Dunsmore of Toronto received
a Valentine in the mail. It was signed, "Your Secret Admirer."
Each year after that, she would receive a card from her mysterious admirer. She continued to receive cards throughout each of
her two marriages. The Valentine arrived late only once—in
1968. That year, the greeting came in July; her admirer
explained that he had been ill. The cards were postmarked from
several foreign countries, including Sweden, France, Australia,
South Africa, China and Japan. On the morning of Meryl's
funeral in July 1988, 60 years after she had received her first
anonymous Valentine, a bouquet of white lilies and yellow chrysanthemums was discovered on the steps of the funeral home.
Attached was a card that said, "Rest in peace, my Valentine."

Valentines by Chance

In 1938, David Ray's cousin asked him to deliver a Valentine's
card to a young woman named Florence. Ray took the card to
Florence, and the young woman was smitten—not by Ray's
cousin, though. Florence and David soon began dating. David
proposed a year later, and the couple were married in 1943.
Seventy years later, their love for each other is still strong.

There Is No Other Valentine

Wanda Addington developed a crush on the teenaged Karl Cates
when she was just a little girl. When she got a bit older, the still-
smitten teenager gave a Valentine's card to the boy of her
dreams. She suggested that the two exchange the card each year
until one or the other got married. This was before the outbreak
of World War II. The two continued to exchange the card
throughout the war. Over the years, Karl began to return
Wanda's affection, and the couple married in 1946 after the war
ended. They were married for 52 years until Karl died in 1998.

During that time, they continued to exchange that same Valentine's card: one year Wanda would send the card to Karl, the next year Karl would send it back to Wanda.

Oh, Valentine, My Valentine,
I've sailed the ocean blue,
Yet never in this life of mine,
Found one to equal you.

(from a late 19th-century Valentine)

Spreading the Love

Sometimes people go the extra mile to make others (and not just those closest to them) feel special on Valentine's Day.

Every Girl Should Feel Special on Valentine's Day

Christian Leos, a junior at Collegiate High School in Corpus Christi, Texas, gave each of the 76 girls in his junior year a rose for Valentine's Day 2013. The young man was the apple of every girl's eye that day. That is a boy with a truly sweet heart!

Classmates Who Care

Instead of exchanging cards on Valentine's Day 2013, the students at Our Lady's Convent Girls' High School in Kochi, India, decided to help out a classmate in need. The home of a fellow student's family in Chellanam had burnt to the ground. The students all donated the money that they would have spent on cards and gifts for Valentine's Day to help the family rebuild their house. This was truly a gift from the heart.

The Loving Mayor of Linton

For Valentine's Day 2013, John Wilkes, mayor of Linton, Indiana, purchased 100 red carnations. Then he dressed in a tuxedo and walked throughout the downtown district of the city handing out a flower to every woman he saw. What a beautiful thing to do!

Learning to Love

In 2013, prison wardens at Kirikiri Prison in Lagos, Nigeria, hosted a Valentine's Day banquet for their female inmates. The prisoners were allowed to dress up for the occasion, and many of them performed in the evening's talent show. Prison officials said that the event was part of the rehabilitation of the inmates, the idea being that the inmates need to experience love in order to know how to show it to others when they are released from prison.

Well Wishes from the World

Carolyn Hastings, a six-year-old kindergarten student from Knoxville, Tennessee, was diagnosed with polymyositis, a rare auto-immune disorder, in late 2007. Her teacher, Elisha Brown, wanted to do something to cheer up the little girl, who was undergoing treatments at Cincinnati Children's Hospital. Brown decided to try to collect 1000 Valentine's cards for the sick child and was amazed at the response. When Carolyn returned to the school to celebrate the holiday with her classmates, she found 13,000 Valentines from Australia, Canada, Finland and across the U.S. waiting for her! She enlisted the help of her classmates in opening the many cards.

Playing Cupid for Charity

Evange Epa, who won Australia's 2013 Gold Coast Young Citizen of the Year Award, went around the campus of Bond University, where he is an architecture student, serenading students and selling roses and cupcakes on Valentine's Day. The money he raised ($1770AU) he donated to a charity in the Solomon Islands—a truly altruistic act of love.

Random Act of Kindness

A college student in Pittsburg, Pennsylvania, took his sweetheart out to a fancy restaurant to celebrate Valentine's Day 2013. The couple had a lovely evening at the pricey establishment. When the young man went to pay the bill, he got a surprise—it had already been paid! He was handed a comment card from the restaurant on which someone (the man suspects an elderly couple that had been sitting nearby) had written: "Random act of kindness. [T]he only request is that someday you pay it forward. In the meantime, enjoy your youth, enjoy friendship, enjoy love. Be good to each other and good luck." The man says he plans to do the same for some other random couple one day.

A Teddy Bear to Show We Care

Since 2008, Taylor Larson has been organizing an annual drive to collect money to buy teddy bears to give to the children who are patients at the Children's Hospital of Illinois in Preoria. Every child receives a teddy bear on Valentine's Day. Extra bears are saved and handed out to children who are admitted during the rest of the year. Taylor was only eight years old during her first teddy bear drive.

DID YOU KNOW?

A large heart sculpture composed entirely of boards from boardwalks in New York and New Jersey destroyed by Hurricane Sandy was assembled in New York's Times Square in time for Valentine's Day 2013.

America's Valentine Phantoms

The Valentine Phantom struck for the first time in 1976 in Portland, Maine. Residents of Portland awoke on Valentine's Day to find sheets of paper with red hearts printed on them posted throughout the town. Every year since then, the phantom has returned, expanding to include Valentine's banners and flags.

In 2002, a Valentine Phantom struck in another community. This time, it was Montpelier, Vermont. The Montpelier Valentine Phantom often includes a love poem written inside the red hearts. In 2007, sculptured hearts appeared for the first time. When the state of Vermont legalized same-sex marriages on September 1, 2009, posters of a rainbow-colored heart appeared across Montpelier in imitation of the Valentine Phantom.

Around the same time that the Valentine Phantom moved into Montpelier, another Valentine Phantom popped up across the country in Boulder, Colorado, where this mysterious character has been dubbed the Kissing Bandit.

In 2012, the phenomenon spread to Bangor, Maine. The Bangor Valentine Phantom has taken to taping a heart-shaped lollipop on the Valentine's Day posters.

No one knows whether these phantoms are individuals or groups, but few people complain about their activities, seeing them as just another way to spread the love on Valentin's Day.

Valentine's Day Love Bombings

Cornwall's Graffiti Grannies
The English county of Cornwall has a group of elderly women who enjoy getting together in secret and planning ways to spread a little love and joy in their local communities. Known as the Graffiti Grannies, these women come up with an occasion and a theme, and then they each knit suitable decorations for the event. In 2013, the group chose the community of Porthleven, and the occasion was Valentine's Day. The residents of Porthleven awoke on February 14 to find that their town had been decorated overnight with knitted hearts and pompoms in red and pink. It created a very festive atmosphere and brought a smile to many people's faces.

Sheepish Heart Bomb Day
Meredith of the blog "One Sheepish Girl" organized a Valentine's Day heart bombing in 2013. She proposed that her readers and fellow knitters each knit a heart or chain of

hearts and hang it up anonymously somewhere in their community on Valentine's Day to share some love with a stranger. The knitters attached the hashtag #sheepishheartbomb to their piece of work, and the finder could enter the tag into Twitter or Instagram to view other heart bombs. It was a nice way to spread the love.

IN THE NAME OF LOVE: CHARITABLE EVENTS AND AWARENESS CAMPAIGNS

Preparing for a Lifelong Love

True Love Waits

In 1993, youth minister Richard Ross of Nashville, Tennessee, founded True Love Waits. The group is for young people who wish to remain celibate until marriage. Members take pledges to remain chaste from that day forward until united in holy matrimony. There are chapters on high school and college campuses throughout the U.S. It has also spread to other countries, including Canada and South Africa. True Love Waits actively asserts its message through advertising campaigns, merchandise sales and proselytizing. In 1997, True Love Waits held its first Valentine's Day Vision, in which groups hung displays of members' pledge cards on their school campuses. Various chapters of the group continue to hold awareness events every Valentine's Day.

Getting Our Hearts Right

In the lead-up to Valentine's Day 2013, the University of
Arkansas' System Division of Agriculture launched its Getting
Our Hearts Right campaign. The result of extensive research,
this campaign revealed the three barriers to conflict-free relationships—a negative attitude, combined with a lack of humility and
compassion for self and others. The campaign included an online
workbook for those who wanted to prepare for the annual day of
love by learning to practice humility, compassion and positivity.

Freedom to Marry

On Valentine's Day 2011, the American coalition Freedom to
Marry, a group that promotes the legalization of same-sex marriages, launched their Why Marriage Matters educational campaign. Valentine's Day is a popular day for gay and lesbian couples
to protest for the legalization of same-sex marriages. Mock public
weddings on Valentine's Day are a common form of protest.

Those who oppose same-sex marriages also sometimes use
Valentine's Day to promote their beliefs. In 2013, the owner of
a Subway franchise in Angers, France, used the company's
Valentine's Day promotion to express his opinion about the proposed legalization of gay marriage in France. Subway had
a Valentine's Day deal for couples, but this owner put up a sign
saying that the deal was limited to heterosexual couples only, creating quite an uproar. Once word got back to company headquar-
ters, the franchise owner had his business immediately shut down.

DID YOU KNOW?

February 7–14 is National Marriage Week in 20 countries,
including the U.S., Britain, Australia, Germany, Italy, Romania,
Bulgaria and the Czech Republic.

Run for the Love of It

Every year, various charities capitalize on the spirit of love by holding fundraising events and runs on Valentine's Day.

Cupid's Undie Run

Cupid's Undie Run is an annual American charity event raising funds for the Children's Tumor Foundation. Runners complete the one-mile run dressed in nothing but their underwear. The event is growing with new cities hosting a run every year. It has even expanded to Australia, where a run was held in Sydney.

The North Shore Cupid's Love Dash

The North Shore Cupid's Love Dash is an annual charity run in Highland Park, Michigan. Participants can partake in either the 5K or 10K run. Upon registration, each person includes their status, either Cupid's Sweethearts (for those in a relationship), Cupid's Singletons (for those looking for love) or Cupid's Lone Solo (for those happy to remain single). En route, runners can stop and enjoy a candy break at two pit stops: Cupid's Chocolate Bliss and Cupid's Candy Oasis. The event raises money for a variety of charities.

The Cupid 5K

The Cupid 5K was held in Seattle, Washington, on Valentine's Day 2013. The charity event raised money and awareness for the A21 Campaign, which fights sex trafficking and slavery. Participants signed up to be part of one of two groups—the Lovers and the Haters (for Anti-Valentine's Day people)—and took part in the charity race and after-party in holiday-themed attire.

Healthy Hearts

In ancient times, the heart was believed to be the center of the intellect as well as emotions. This is how it came to be associated with love and, hence, Valentine's Day. In recent years, there has been a trend to highlight heart health in February to tie in with all the Valentine's Day heart symbolism.

♥ The American government made February National Heart Month.

♥ Every year, the American Heart Association runs an anti-smoking campaign the week of Valentine's Day called Save a Sweet Heart. It is aimed at high school students.

♥ The U.S. Centers for Disease Control promote awareness of heart disease by offering Valentine's Day e-cards such as, "Valentine, dear Valentine, My heart beats just for you. To keep our hearts beating, Let's walk a mile or two."

♥ The father of Daniel Littleboy of Norwich, England, passed away from a heart attack on February 14, 2010. A year later, Daniel announced that he was going to bike 1800 miles from Norwich to its twin cities of Novi Sad, Serbia, then Koblenz, Germany, then Rouen, France, and finally back to Norwich, all to raise money for Heart Research U.K.

♥ Swim for Your Heart is an international effort to promote heart health through swimming. People are asked to swim for a mile or an hour on Valentine's Day. Those unable to swim are invited to make a donation to a local heart-health program. In 2013, people in 28 countries participated.

♥ Macy's, the American department store chain, joined up with the American Heart Association's Go Red for Women: Support Women's Heart Health campaign for February 2013. People could post one of 11 red-themed images on Facebook, Twitter, Pinterest or Instagram. For each post, Macy's donated $2 to the association.

♥ For Valentine's Day 2013, Bart's Pathology Museum at the Queen Mary, University of London, offered an alternative way to spend the day. Visitors were treated to demonstrations of a variety of heart surgeries with the aid of videos and computers. A lecture was given about the benefits of wine and chocolate for the heart. Four cakes shaped like the human heart were raffled off.

♥ On Valentine's Day 2013, three-year-old Trinity Lazo of Gastonia, North Carolina, received the greatest gift of love possible: life. Trinity suffered from a disorder that prevented her heart from being able to transmit oxygen to the rest of her body. Without a new heart, Trinity was going to die. Thanks to another family's priceless gift and the work of doctors at the Cincinnati Children's Hospital, Trinity received a new heart and a new chance at life.

You Are a Breath of Fresh Air

Heart associations are not the only groups to use Valentine's Day as a means of promoting better health. Lung associations have also jumped on the bandwagon.

♥ The British Lung Association released a pamphlet for Valentine's Day 2010 called "Sex and Breathlessness." The pamphlet contained numerous suggestions to help couples express their love for each other physically where one person has lung disease. Suggestions included alternatives to sexual intercourse, such as kissing, hugging and cuddling, as well as positions for sexual intercourse that would place the least amount of stress and pressure on the sufferer's lungs.

♥ The Lung Association of Nova Scotia offers Country Heart Seals to those who donate to the charity. The heart seals arrive in the mail at the end of January or beginning of February—just in time for Valentine's Day.

♥ The website for the American Lung Association offers shopping advice for anyone buying a Valentine's Day gift for someone with asthma: avoid flowers with strong fragrances; try to buy pollen-free flowers; stay away from scented gifts; go for dinner at a smoke-free restaurant.

♥ Dr. Ronnie Delany, former Olympic runner and gold medalist, teamed up with the Irish Lung Health Alliance to promote healthy lungs for Valentine's Day 2012 in a campaign called Love Your Lungs.

DID YOU **KNOW?**

February 14 is also National Donor Day in the U.S. for organ donors.

Cupid and Cancer

St. Valentine's Day Hair Massacure

The St. Valentine's Hair Massacure was first held in 2003 in Edmonton, Alberta. The event was the brainchild of Tammy and Gordon MacDonald, whose daughter Kali was a cancer patient. Kali had undergone extensive chemotherapy, which had resulted in the loss of her hair—a devastating occurrence for most girls and women. The purpose of the St. Valentine's Hair Massacure was to invite people to voluntarily shave their heads to show solidarity with cancer patients, as well as to create an awareness of the various impacts cancer has on the lives of those suffering from it.

In 2006, a new twist was added, whereby participants were asked to dye their hair pink for the days or weeks leading up to Valentine's Day. The pink hair attracted people's attention and created a greater public awareness. That year, the event made the *Guiness Book of World Records* for the most heads shaved (840) under one roof in a single day.

Although the Hair Massacure didn't begin as a fundraiser, donations poured into the event. Since 2010, the St. Valentine's Day Hair Massacure has raised over a million dollars annually, with the proceeds being divided between Make-a-Wish Northern Alberta, the Stollery Children's Hospital Foundation and the Ronald McDonald House in Edmonton.

Kali MacDonald battled leukemia for three years. In 2003, when she was five, Kali's cancer went into remission and has remained so ever since.

A Valentine's Day Wedding

Singing sensation Justin Bieber made six-year-old Avalanna Routh's Valentine's Day wish come true. The Boston girl suffered from a rare form of cancer called atypical teratoid rhabdoid tumor, or ATRT. A huge Justin Bieber fan, the child desperately wanted to meet her favorite singer, so her parents posted her wish on Facebook. Learning of the girl's desire, Bieber flew the family to meet him in Manhattan for Valentine's Day 2012, which he spent playing board games and hairdresser with the little girl. The two even had a mock wedding, much to Avalanna's delight. What a great gift. Sadly, Avalanna passed away eight months later.

Love Notes

In 2012, the American Cancer Society launched its Love Notes Around the World campaign. The project is designed to collect Valentine's cards from people all over the world and to distribute them to cancer patients and survivors as well as their families. The Valentine's cards provide a bit of joy and let people know that they are not alone, that there are people who care.

A Room Full of Roses

In 2013, 11-year-old Kanesha Greer of Sweetwater, Oklahoma, was diagnosed with osteosarcoma, a type of bone cancer, and given only a 10 percent chance of surviving. As her illness progressed, she told her mother that her wish was to have a house full of roses for Valentine's Day. As her daughter grew sicker, Kanesha's mother created a Facebook page called Team Nesha on which she posted her daughter's wish and stated that, given the gravity of her daughter's illness, the family would be celebrating Valentine's Day early, on February 1. Roses were soon pouring into the Greer household from florists all over the state, making Kanesha's Valentine's Day wish come true. Kanesha passed away soon afterward on March 3.

Monk's Makeovers

Breast cancer survivor Caroline Monk knows the effects that chemotherapy and surgery can have on the self-esteem of women suffering from cancer. To help lift the spirits of these women, Monk organizes various spa and beauty events and asks businesses to donate their time and services. For Valentine's Day 2012, she arranged for seven cancer patients in London to receive makeovers to prepare for an evening of fun on the town. The women had their make-up and hair or wigs done, received new outfits and shoes and were taken via a limo to a party with celebrities.

K.I.S.S.

For Valentine's Day 2012, Ovarian Cancer Australia launched its K.I.S.S. campaign to promote awareness of the disease. K.I.S.S. stands for "Know the Important Signs and Symptoms," and Australians were invited to email an informational K.I.S.S. to women they loved on Valentine's Day.

Bags of Cheer

Every year since 2000, volunteers make piles of handmade
Valentine's cards to be distributed to the adult cancer patients at
the University of Michigan Comprehensive Cancer Center. Each
patient is given a bag full of cards on Valentine's Day. The volunteers who make the cards include school children, elderly residents of nursing homes, prison inmates and others.

Spreading Awareness: HIV/AIDS
and Valentine's Day

Because Valentine's Day is a time for people who are in love to
express their love and affection for each other, it is also a time of
increased sexual activity. Governments, companies and charities
with a vested interest in sex and its consequences recognize this
fact. Durex, a major manufacturer of condoms, reports that
the sale of condoms increases by up to 30 percent at this time
of year. Other reports show that March is the month with the
highest sale of home pregnancy tests. February 13 is International
Condom Awareness Day.

Many organizations now hold events on or near February 14
that aim to create an awareness of the HIV/AIDS epidemic, to
educate the public on ways to prevent the spread of the illness
and to lessen discrimination against those who already have the
disease.

♥ Since 1993, Lisa Myers has organized Valentines for AIDS,
a silent auction in Boise, Idaho, whose proceeds go to SNAP
(Safety Net for AIDS Program). The event allows people to
discuss and learn about the disease, as well as to support
those affected by it in a fun-filled, party atmosphere.

♥ In 2010, Godiva Chocolates joined with the Elton John
AIDS Foundation in a Valentine's Day fundraiser. The chocolate manufacturer produced a limited edition box of chocolates called True Love Gold Heart. Proceeds from the sale of
the chocolates in the amount of $200,000 were presented by
the winner of the 2010 Godiva Valentine's Day Sweepstakes
to Elton John at a benefit event.

♥ On Valentine's Day 2012, members of the Rwanda Media
Network against HIV/AIDS targeted youths in a campaign
to promote safe sex. Members hosted talk shows on the
radio and visited local hot spots to talk to youths, who were
encouraged to either abstain from sex or to wear a condom.

♥ The Valentine's Day Walk held on February 14, 2013, in
Accra, Ghana, was a charity event to raise awareness of
HIV/AIDS and to encourage people to wear condoms.

♥ The Bulgarian government ran an HIV/AIDS awareness
and testing campaign on Valentine's Day 2013. Information
brochures and condoms were handed out by volunteers in
Sophia, while mobile testing sites were set up throughout
the city.

♥ In 2013, Elton John teamed up with Chinese artist Ai
Weiwei to promote a greater understanding of HIV/AIDS
and to lessen the stigmatization of those who suffer from the
illness. The campaign featured an educational video showing
a number of celebrities pricking their fingers. The video was
shown in New York's Times Square, London's Picadilly
Circus and Kiev's Independence Square starting on
February 14. The campaign was called Love Is in My Blood.

The Vagina Monologues and the Rise of V-Day

In 1994, in New York City, playwright Eve Ensler first performed *The Vagina Monologues*, a series of soliloquies on women's experiences "down there." It was a phenomenal success. People flocked to see it. Women began to talk about their own experiences with menstruation, menopause, giving birth, consensual and forced sex, female genital mutilation and illness. People became more aware of the prevalence of violence, especially sexual violence, in the lives of women everywhere. In Canada and the U.S., one in every four women will be sexually assaulted sometime in her life.

In 1998, an international campaign called V-Day was created to raise awareness and funds to stop violence against women and girls. The "V" in V-Day stands for victory, Valentine and vagina. Many, though not all, V-Day events are held annually on February 14 and take a wide variety of forms, from presentations of Ensler's famous monologues to marches and rallies, anti-violence workshops and benefit galas. Screenings of the documentaries *Until the Violence Stops* and *What I Want My Words to Do* are also common.

The money raised at these V-Day events is used to fund local women's shelters and rape crisis centers, as well as other projects that work to help women and girls who have been the victims of violence. The V-Day organization itself provides funding world-wide for similar but larger projects, such as opening the first women's shelters in Egypt and Iraq. To date, V-Day has helped to raise awareness and funds in 140 countries.

Since 2002, V-Day has spotlighted specific issues:

- In 2002, the spotlight was on the plight of women in Afghanistan, where the Taliban has deprived them of all rights, creating an environment where acts of violence against women are common and often unpunished.

- In 2003, the spotlight was on First Nations Women. Native American women are 3.5 times more likely to be the victims of violence than other women.

- In 2004, V-Day focused an international spotlight on the unsolved murders of over 400 women and girls over the previous decade in the Mexican city of Juarez. As a result, the state attorney resigned. Unfortunately, the killings remain unsolved.

- The women of war-torn Iraq were the focus of V-Day's 2005 campaign. The American military presence in the country actually lowered the status of women there because of the disruptions caused by the war as well as the extremist reactions of militant Islamic factions within the country.

- In 2006, V-Day joined the efforts of former "comfort women" to obtain an apology and compensation from the Japanese government for the systematic sexual abuse these women suffered at the hands of Japanese soldiers between 1932 and 1945. "Comfort women" were forced or tricked to become sex slaves to Japanese soldiers.

💛 Women living in conflict zones are victims of increased levels of violence. In 2007, V-Day sought to increase international awareness of their suffering.

💛 In 2008, V-Day focused on the tragic losses of women and girls in New Orleans and area as a result of Hurricane Katrina.

💛 2009 and 2010 saw the spotlight turned on the women and girls of the Democratic Republic of Congo, where the incidence of rape is very high and the degree of violence used is often extreme. The building of the City of Joy rape crisis center resulted from this campaign.

💛 The devastating earthquake that hit the small island nation of Haiti brought increased poverty and sexual violence in its wake. In 2011 and 2012, V-Day sought to provide relief to the women and girls living there.

💛 2013 marked the 15th anniversary of V-Day. The spotlight was shone on the horrible statistic that one in three women worldwide will be the victim of physical or sexual violence sometime in her life. The campaign is called One Billion Rising to highlight the huge number of victims, as well as to state that the number will continue to rise if no one does anything to stop the violence. People everywhere were encouraged to rise up on February 14 to show their opposition to violence against women and girls. There were 5800 events worldwide.

DID YOU KNOW?

The San Francisco Board of Supervisors declared February 14, 2013, One Billion Rising Day in their city.

Care or Control?

Actress Helena Bonham Carter, a longtime supporter of Refuge, a British domestic violence charity, launched the group's 2010 Valentine's Day Care or Control? campaign. The educational program featured four posters showing what seemed to be typical Valentine's Day teddy bears holding hearts. However, the messages on the hearts were sinister rather than sweet (e.g., ONLY YOU make me do this). The posters highlighted four aspects of controlling behavior—blame, charm, isolation and jealousy.

Home Is Where the Heart Is

Buffalo Hearts Old Buildings

The group Buffalo Young Preservationists in Buffalo, Ohio, works actively to promote the preservation of old buildings and historic sites in the city. They chose Valentine's Day 2013 to draw attention to the sad state of four abandoned homes. The group spent weeks constructing large Valentines out of construction paper with labels such as "Love Me, Don't Leave Me" and "True Love is about Building Up, Not Tearing Down." Group members attached the Valentines to the four chosen buildings on Valentine's Day, garnishing media attention and initiating a dialogue with city officials.

For the Love of Freedom

Hundreds of young Iraqis joined the Spring Uprising on Valentine's Day 2011. Wearing red outfits and carrying roses and balloons, they gathered in Baghdad to protest government greed. They chose Valentine's Day as a fitting time to show their love for their country and for their fellow Iraqis.

Women of Zimbabwe Arise

Dressed in red and white, the members of Women of Zimbabwe Arise (WOZA) have been gathering every Valentine's Day since 2003 in Harare and Bulawayo to spread awareness about government oppression in Zimbabwe. The women want access to better health care and education. They also want the people to have more of a say in politics.

Under the rule of President Robert Mugabe and the Zimbabwe African National Union-Patriotic Front (ZANU-PF), the citizens of Zimbabwe have suffered dreadfully for the past 25 years. So on Valentine's Day, members of WOZA distribute red paper roses and cards that encourage people to stand up for their rights and to be more loving toward one another. The theme changes each year: in 2006, it was "Bread and Roses"; in 2013, it was "One Love."

The Zimbabwe government does not like these demonstrations, and arrests are common. Magodonga Mahlangu, the leader of WOZA and recipient of the 2009 Robert F. Kennedy Human Rights Award, has been arrested several times. In 2013, the police in Harare fired canisters of tear gas at the protesters, while the police in Bulawayo beat up 50 of the women.

LOVE MAKES THE WORLD GO 'ROUND: THE HOLIDAY AROUND THE GLOBE

France, Land of Romance

Valentine's Day in France, the birthplace of troubadours and courtly romance, is a holiday reserved for adults. The celebration of Valentine's Day in France stretches back at least to the beginning of the 15th century and has been going strong ever since.

The 17th-century French princess Christine Marie (1606–1663) referred to her palace near Turin as the Valentine. She held a Valentine's Day party there every year, during which the ladies drew names for the gentleman who was to be their Valentine for that year. The only exception was the princess herself, who chose the man she wanted to be her Valentine. At the many dances held throughout the year, the gentlemen were expected to present their Valentine with a small bouquet, while at tournaments the ladies were to pay for the outfitting of their Valentine's horse. The man who won the tournament presented his prize to his Valentine.

By the 1950s, French magazines were featuring articles that advised women on how to communicate with a man on Valentine's Day through the food with which she presented him. An apple or a pear meant that the young man's attentions were welcome; an egg told him that she had no interest in him. According to the articles, this was a tradition that dated back centuries.

Like many countries, France regularly issues special Valentine's Day stamps. France's 1985 Valentine's Day stamp was a reproduction of Raymond Peynet's painting "St. Valentine" and shows a pair of lovers in the woods with a dove and little cupids putting letters in a heart-shaped mailbox. Every year since 2003, France has issued two heart-shaped stamps for Valentine's Day. The designs change annually.

Every year around Valentine's Day, the French city of Roquemaure, home of the Lovers' Fountain, holds its Festival of the Kiss. The festival is said to commemorate the arrival of the remains of St. Valentine to the city in 1868. A parade is held and street performers abound. The streets are renamed with the names of France's best-known fictional lovers. At the Festival of the Handles of Love, people gather together to sing love songs.

On Valentine's Day 2010, as part of its 150th anniversary celebrations, the French seaside resort town of Deauville invited people to re-enact the famous love scene from the end of the 1966 romance movie *A Man and A Woman*. In the scene, a woman named Anne (played by Anouk Aimée) sits on a bench on the beach. A man named Jean-Louis (played by Jean-Louis Trintignant) has driven all night to find her. He sees her on the beach and runs to her. Noticing him, she goes toward him and the two embrace. The man twirls her in the air in his arms. Hundreds of couples of all ages showed up to recreate the scene. They did so several times and then had the opportunity to switch partners if they so chose.

DID YOU KNOW?

The residents of the cities of Valencia in Spain, Valence in France and Valenza in Italy are known as Valentines.

Italian Lovers

Valentine's Day in Verona

The city of Verona, Italy, was the home of Shakespeare's ill-fated lovers Romeo and Juliet. Many people do not realize that Shakespeare's play was based upon a real rivalry between two powerful families—the Montecchi (or Montagues) and Capuleti (or Capulets)—in the 13th century. Their respective palaces still stand and are now known as Romeo's House and Juliet's House. Juliet's House is now a luxury hotel. The room with her famous balcony can be rented, and couples can be married on the balcony. The entrance to the house is covered with love graffiti. There is a statue of Juliet in the courtyard, and it is said that if you rub her right breast, you will be lucky in love.

The tragic lovers are big business in Verona, so it is no surprise that the city does much to promote the celebration of Valentine's Day. The city holds an annual contest for the best love letter sent to Juliet. The winner of the love letter contest is announced on February 14, and the prize is presented at Juliet's house. The contest is sponsored by the Juliet Club.

Red heart-shaped balloons are handed out in Verona in the week leading up to Valentine's Day. A large red heart-shaped carpet is laid out in the Piazza dei Signori. Red heart-shaped confetti is thrown from towers throughout Verona at random times on Valentine's Day. Among the confetti are ballots for a love lottery.

DID YOU  KNOW?

Shakespeare makes no mention of Valentine's Day in *Romeo and Juliet*. Valentine's Day is, however, mentioned in *A Midsummer Night's Dream* and *Hamlet*:

> *Good morrow! 'Tis St. Valentine's Day*
> *All in the morning betime,*
> *And I a maid at yon window,*
> *To be your Valentine!*

> (Ophelia in Shakespeare's *Hamlet*)

Chocolate Kisses in Italy

Chocolate is the customary gift of lovers in Italy as in much of the world. However, in Italy, a special type of chocolate is given on Valentine's Day. Called *baci perugina* (*baci* means "kisses" in Italian), these sweet treats come wrapped in tender messages of love.

The love messages found wrapped around baci perugina are said to have originated in the alleged love affair between Luisa Spagnoli and Giovanni Biutoni. Luisa, her husband and Giovanni were business partners who owned a chocolate-making business. The story goes that Luisa and Giovanni became lovers and communicated through messages wrapped inside the foil wrappers of chocolates they made.

Hogs and Kisses in Germany

Valentine's Day has been celebrated in Germany only since the end of World War II. However, Germans have fully embraced the holiday since then. The day, which is for adults only, is marked by the exchange of gifts and cards as well as going on dates. A popular gift in Germany is a large heart-shaped gingerbread cookie decorated with icing flowers and a tender message. Also filling the shops in Germany at this time are pigs—figurine pigs, stuffed animal pigs, marzipan pigs. Pigs are everywhere on Valentine's Day! Why? To Germans, pigs represent good luck and lust, and the suggestive poses of many of the animals on display indicate that the giver is hoping to have a certain sort of luck with the recipient that day!

DID YOU  KNOW?

At the beginning of February 2008, a litter of piglets was born on a farm in Gloucestershire. One of the piglets was born with a heart-shaped patch near its rump. His owners named him Valentine.

Pushing Flowers in the Netherlands

The tiny European nation of the Netherlands produces 60 percent of the flowers marketed worldwide, so it's no wonder that the country's National Organization of Florists sought to make the celebration of Valentine's Day a Dutch tradition. In 1949, the organization first awarded a bouquet of flowers on Valentine's Day to individuals who had made an exceptional contribution to society. It was hoped that doing so would boost flower sales within the country, which were rather low at the time. Valentine's Day, however, was slow to catch on with the Dutch. The sale of Valentine's cards is a recent occurrence, with the cards appearing on shop shelves only in the last decade. Today, Valentine's Day in the Netherlands is more a day for expressing one's appreciation for others rather than a day dedicated to love and romance.

DID YOU  **KNOW?**

In 2005, the Netherlands produced an ingenious Valentine's Day stamp showing two hearts lying on their sides facing each other. They looked like lips kissing.

Q: Why did the skunk send his girlfriend a bouquet of flowers on Valentine's Day?

A: He was scent-imental!

Scandinavian Sweethearts

Egg-stra Fun in Denmark

While Danish men give their sweethearts gifts of candy and flowers on Valentine's Day much like men in other parts of the world, the flowers are usually snowdrops rather than roses. Danish men also give their lady friends a uniquely Danish gift known as *Gaekkebrev*. *Gaekkebrev* are humorous poems that men give anonymously to women on Valentine's Day. At the end of the poem, the man gives the woman a clue as to his identity— dots representing the number of letters in the man's name. The woman has till Easter to guess the identity of the sender. If she guesses correctly, the man must give her a decorated egg on Easter Day. If she is unable to guess who has sent the poem to her, she must prepare an Easter egg that the sender will come to claim, thereby revealing his identity to her finally.

Heartfelt Wishes from Sweden

Valentine's Day has only really been celebrated in Sweden since the 1990s, though Swedish florists have been promoting the holiday since the 1960s. Compared to the U.S. or Britain, Valentine's Day in Sweden is decidedly low-key. Couples might exchange cards or gifts (flowers and jelly hearts are popular), but excessive commercialism surrounding the holiday is not seen. Nonetheless, the day is a boon for some sectors of the business world in Sweden, with the sale of cosmetics and flowers for Valentine's Day being second only to those sold for Mother's Day.

In 2013, the Swedish police decided to get in the spirit of All Hearts' Day (what Valentine's Day is called in Sweden) and created a humorous guide to showing your love for your local cops. The tips included leaving a flower at the local police station and waving to police officers rather than giving them the finger. Swedes were encouraged to post a nice comment on Facebook or to send in tips regarding lawbreakers. And finally, "Do not commit burglary. (There's no better way to say "I love you" to a police officer). If you cannot resist and are forced to commit burglary, be sure to leave some fingerprints or DNA at the crime scene. (Another good way to tell the police, "I love you, but I am afraid to take the first step, so I want you to search me up instead.)"

Battle of the Saints: Eastern Europe

Not every Christian nation has celebrated February 14 as the feast day of St. Valentine or has celebrated it as a day of love. Some countries, particularly those who follow the Orthodox Church, have other saints who represent love or celebrate February 14 as the feast day of a different saint. The introduction of Valentine's Day, with its western, commercialized brand of love, is not always welcomed with open arms. The result is often a rift in the population, with some members following the old traditions and others embracing the new global culture. In still other cases, people celebrate both occasions.

Bulgaria

In Bulgaria, St. Valentine's Day is a new holiday, having been around for only 15 years. It competes with the ancient Bulgarian holiday of St. Trifon the Martyr, which is a day for ensuring a successful year of growing and harvesting grapes and making wine. Farmers perform a ritual first pruning of the vines. The farmers' wives distribute round loaves of bread. The fruit trees that have stood barren all winter are threatened with being cut down if they don't produce in the coming year. It is customary for Bulgarians to drink lots of wine on this day.

Greece

In 2000, Archbishop Christodoulos of the Greek Orthodox Church called on his countrymen to ignore St. Valentine's Day and to celebrate their love for their partners one day earlier, on the feast day of St. Akilas and St. Proskili, a married couple who invited the Apostle Paul into their home.

Slovenia

The people of Slovenia have little need for Valentine's Day. Slovenians already have three days on which they celebrate their love for each other—St. Vincent's Day on February 22, St. Gregory's Day on March 12, and St. Anthony's Day on June 13. Of course, having those three days has not stopped some Slovenians from adding a fourth day to the list. After all, you can never have too much loving.

 **DID YOU KNOW?**

February 14 is also the feast day of St. Adolph of Osnabruck.

Red, White and Black: Japan and South Korea

Valentine's Day

Valentine's Day was introduced to Japan in 1936 by the Japanese chocolate company Morozoff Ltd. The company hoped to target foreigners living in the country. By the 1950s, other companies had followed suit, and by the end of the decade, Valentine's Day was being celebrated among the Japanese themselves. The new holiday eventually found its way to South Korea as well.

In Japan, Valentine's Day is a day for women to give chocolates to the men in their lives. In the 1970s, chocolate makers began producing different types of chocolates to convey specific meanings to the recipients. There are currently four types of chocolate gifts available:

1) True Feeling Chocolates—These chocolates are reserved for that special man in a woman's life and may be homemade. For Valentine's Day 2013, KS Design Lab in Tokyo, Japan, offered women the chance to give a truly unique chocolate. Women could get a full-body scan, which was then used to create a mold of the woman's face to be used to make a chocolate gift.

2) Friend Chocolates—These chocolates are meant for a woman's female friends and are a relatively new variety of Valentine's Day gift.

3) Obligation Chocolates—These chocolates are given to the men in a woman's life who play an important but non-romantic role, such as fathers, brothers, colleagues and classmates.

4) Ultra-obligation Chocolates—These are the lowest grade of chocolates and are reserved for those men in a woman's life whom she does not particularly like, such as a troublesome co-worker or unfriendly classmate.

In South Korea, Valentine's Day is also a day for women to give gifts to men. However, the practice is more limited than in Japan, with many women only giving chocolate to their boyfriend or husband.

DID YOU  KNOW?

"Valentine Kiss" is the most popular Valentine's Day song in Japan. It was released just in time for the big day in 1986 by Sayuri Kokushō. Another well-liked song is Yumi Matsutoya's "Valentine's Radio."

White Day

In 1977, the Japanese candy company Ishimuramanseido tried to introduce a day on which men could reciprocate and give women gifts of marshmallows. Within the year, the idea was seized upon by the Japanese chocolate manufacturers, and White Day was created. Celebrated on March 14, this is the day on which men give gifts to the women from whom they received chocolates a month earlier. The gifts given by the men are not limited to chocolates, however. They are also generally two or three times more expensive than what they themselves received.

White seems a strange color to have been associated with the day, for although white conveys purity in the West, in Asian countries, the color is traditionally associated with death. Nonetheless, white was the color chosen, and white-colored presents (or at least gifts presented in white boxes) are given on this day. White chocolate is also the most common type for women to receive on this day.

In South Korea, school children give gifts of candy to their classmates on both Valentine's Day and White Day, regardless of their gender.

DID YOU  KNOW?

In Taiwan, people also celebrate Valentine's Day and White Day. However, the roles are reversed, with men giving gifts to women on Valentine's Day and women returning the favor on White Day. For Valentine's Day 2012, 101 Taiwanese men had messages of love prominently displayed on Taipei's tallest skyscraper. The proclamation cost each man thousands of dollars.

Black Day
In South Korea, a third Valentine's Day–related holiday has evolved. Black Day is celebrated on April 14. This day is reserved for single men and women who did not receive a gift on either Valentine's Day or White Day. These men and women gather together in restaurants to eat a special dish of noodles smothered in a black bean sauce (hence the name of the day).

Valentine's Day in the Philippines

I Do, I Do, I Do
All across the Philippines, mass weddings are held on Valentine's Day. The ceremonies are generally funded by either the government or a charitable organization to allow many Filipino couples, who could not otherwise afford the cost of the ceremony, to marry. In 2013, over 3000 couples tied the knot in these Valentine's Day mass weddings.

Candy vs. Condoms
On Valentine's Day 2013, members of Pro-Life Philippines and Filipinos for Life handed out bags of candy to pedestrians as a reminder that Valentine's Day is about love, not lust, and that people should wait until marriage to have sex. The action was

a direct response to the free distribution of condoms by supporters of the reproductive health law, which allows access to free contraception and sexual education.

The Postman Delivers
In the Philippines, the post office delivers not only cards and love letters on Valentine's Day but also chocolates and flowers. In addition, the government issues special Valentine's Day stamps each year. The four Valentine's Day stamps issued in 2002 revolved around the theme that love knows no bounds, not religious, linguistic or geographic.

Unwanted Gifts
On the evening of February 13, 2005, three bombs exploded in the Philippines. Four people were killed and 60 wounded when a bomb went off in a passenger bus in Makati City. Another four people were killed and 36 wounded when two more bombs exploded, one at a bus terminal in Davao and another at a mall in General Santos City. Soon after, a member of the Islamic terrorist group Abu Sayyaf claimed responsibility, saying the explosions were the group's Valentine's Day gifts to Filipino president Gloria Macapaga-Arroyo. They said the bombs were payback for the government's poor treatment of Muslims. Four men were later arrested for the bombings. One, Gappal Bannah Asali, turned state witness. The other three men—Gamal Baharan, Angelo Trinidad and Rohmat Abdurrohim—were convicted and received death sentences that were later converted to life in prison after the death penalty was abolished in the Philippines.

DID YOU KNOW?

Filipinos living abroad have taken to sending a singing telegram to their sweetheart back home on Valentine's Day.

Valentine's Day in Thailand

The celebration of Valentine's Day is a relatively new tradition in Thailand, having only really caught on in the last few decades. However, it has become hugely popular among the Thai people. People of all ages participate in the festivities. The country's flower market does a booming business on Valentine's Day, and the government, along with individual companies, has worked hard to promote Thailand as the place for couples to go for a romantic getaway or unique wedding experience.

❤ Elementary school children in Thailand put stickers on their friends' shirts on Valentine's Day.

❤ Thai officials do their best to prevent teenagers from engaging in sexual activity to celebrate Valentine's Day. The city keeps the lights on in Bangkok's parks all night and instituted a 10:00 PM curfew for everyone under the age of 18. The police patrol the cheaper hotels.

❤ In Bangkok, single people make offerings at what has come to be known as Lover's Shrine. Dedicated to the Hindu trinity of Brahma the creator, Vishnu the maintainer and Shiva the destroyer, Thai people believe that by making these offerings on Valentine's Day, they will secure a lifelong love.

❤ Police in Khon Kaen set up a road block on Valentine's Day 2013. Instead of handing out tickets though, the police were handing out roses as well as warnings to motorists caught breaking the law and helmets to motorcyclists without one.

❤ The Swiss designer Chopard launched its Happy White St. Valentine's Watch in 2009. The watch features a floating heart made of 13 small diamonds and a buckle of steel symbolizing forever and was available exclusively at the company's Siam Paragon boutique.

♥ The district of Bang Rak in Bangkok is a very trendy place to get married, especially on Valentine's Day, when couples start lining up outside the district office in the wee hours of the morning. The reason for the area's popularity can be found in its name: Bang Rak means "Village of Love." Couples believe that getting hitched there is a lucky start to their married life. Every year on Valentine's Day, the Bang Rak district office holds a draw and gives one lucky couple a gold marriage certificate.

♥ Since 1996, underwater weddings have been offered to couples at Pak Meng Beach on Valentine's Day. The couples, who must be certified scuba divers, exchange their vows using divers' sign language.

♥ On Valentine's Day 2013, a hugging contest was held in Bangkok. Teams of 14 people had to squeeze into one square meter and hug for 10 minutes.

Celebrating Love in China

Qixi Festival

Way before Valentine's Day arrived in China, there was the festival of love known as Qixi, or the Double Seventh (it falls on the seventh day of the seventh month). Originally a festival for single women or newlyweds, it is increasingly becoming a day to celebrate love between all couples.

The origins of the festival are found in the Chinese folktale about Zhinu (the star Vega) and Niulang (the star Altair). Zhinu was the youngest daughter of the Goddess. One day, she snuck away from her home in the heavens to explore the world below. On her travels on earth, she met the cowherd Niulang. The two fell in love, married and had two children before Zhinu's absence from the heavens was noted and her location discovered. Angry, the Goddess ordered Zhinu to return home, leaving Niulang alone with their children. The cowherd's ox spoke to the grieving man and told him that in order to journey to the heavens to be reunited with his wife, Niulang had to kill the ox and skin it. By wearing the ox's hide, the cowherd would be able to rise to the heavens with his children. The distraught man did as his ox directed and soon had his wife back in his arms. The Goddess, however, did not want her daughter to be paired with a mere mortal and separated the couple by drawing a river (the Milky Way) in the sky between them. A flock of magpies saw the unhappy pair and decided to help them. So every year on the seventh day of the seventh month, a flock of magpies flies to the heavens and makes a bridge across the Milky Way, allowing the couple to be together for one day. The magpie has become a symbol of marital harmony and fidelity in China.

The Double Seventh festival dates back to the Han dynasty (206 BCE–220 CE). Historically, Qixi was a time for young girls to make divinations to see their marital futures. It was also a time when single women could display their prowess in needle-working skills through contests and demonstrations. Needlework was an important domestic duty for women, and being able to show ability in this area increased a woman's chances of finding a husband. Unmarried women made offerings to Zhinu, asking her to increase their chances of attracting a good husband. Newlywed couples also made offerings to Zhinu on this day.

Today, the Qixi festival is mainly celebrated in rural areas of China. In the big cities, it is the Western Valentine's Day that has become the more popular day for love.

Rent-a-Boyfriend

Valentine's Day may be new to China, but the pressure on young women to marry is not. In China, a woman is considered an old maid if she is not married by her 27th birthday—the average age of marriage for women in the West. If a woman has not married by then (or doesn't even have a boyfriend), not only is she shamed but her family is, as well. Young Chinese women have found a new way to respond to this immense societal pressure by renting a boyfriend for special occasions!

Companies offering boyfriends for rent provide their customers with a wide range of services from which to choose, from morning wake-up calls to a dinner or movie date to weekend getaways to her parents' place. What is not offered or allowed are any sexual services. In fact, if a "boyfriend" makes any untoward moves on the client, she can demand a full refund.

These "boyfriends" do not come cheap, but some young Chinese women believe the cost is worth it. By bringing home a suitable young man to meet her family, friends and neighbors on Valentine's Day, the woman is saving her reputation...at least until the next special occasion.

Personal Ads and Matchmaking Events

The pressure to marry is also great for Chinese men. Since the Chinese government instituted the one-child policy in 1980, men in China greatly outnumber women, with male children being more highly valued than girls. This disparity means that single men now have to compete fiercely to find a bride from a reduced pool compared to previous generations. Men need to acquire a house, a vehicle and a good job to even be considered in most cases.

At all times of the year but especially around Valentine's Day and Qixi, single Chinese men and women seek out a variety of means to find a partner. On these days of love, personal ads can be seen plastered all over the streets in major cities, and matchmaking events proliferate. Not only are the men and women themselves posting these ads, but parents are doing so, too.

DID YOU KNOW?

In 2003, certain carriages on the subway trains in Vienna, Austria, were set up as Valentine's Day "flirt cars" to help single people find partners.

Playing Cupid: the Government and Singapore's Singles

For over a decade now, the government of Singapore has been concerned about the country's declining population. Couples are not marrying as young as they once did, nor are they producing as many children. People are spending more time working and less time socializing; they are chasing money rather than love.

To help people to find a spouse, the Singapore government launched a campaign in February 2002 called Romancing Singapore. Every year throughout the month of February, the government and private sector businesses promote romance and dating through advertising campaigns and matchmaking/dating events. In 2006, the government launched a million-dollar Partner Connection Fund, which gives grants to businesses that promote dating services.

During the month of February, signs of Valentine's Day can be found throughout the country. Merchants hawk teddy bears, floral bouquets, balloons, chocolate and candy. Restaurants and hotels offer special deals. Dating agencies have a variety of events, some for couples and some for singles hoping to meet someone special. In Singapore, love is not only in the air in February—it is everywhere.

DID YOU  KNOW?

In Mongolia, Valentine's Day is known as Couples' Day.

Valentine's Day in India: a Clash of Cultures

Traditionally in India, one of the most populous countries in the world, marriage is not about two people in love deciding to spend their lives together. Marriage is about creating a social and economic bond between two families. In the past, the two people who were marrying did not even meet until the day of their wedding. Today, couples may be allowed to get to know each other somewhat by going out on a few dates before committing to a marriage.

Over the past generation, however, the Western notion of love matches has created ripples of contention throughout India as the ways of the past clash with the new ideas being imported into the country in this era of globalization.

Valentine's Day is a focal point for the conflicts between the young, Westernized urbanites and the sometimes extreme fundamentalist Hindu and Muslim groups and older, more conservative members of the community. In 2009, Pramod Mutalik, leader of the fundamentalist Hindu group Sri Ram Sena, threatened to force any unmarried couples caught celebrating Valentine's Day to wed. In response, thousands of women across India mailed pink panties to the group's head office in Bangalore. The Hindu fundamentalist groups Vishwa Hindu Parishad and Bajrang Dal also oppose Valentine's Day celebrations. Members of Shiv Sena, another Hindu extremist group, attack unmarried couples on Valentine's Day, raid stores and burn piles of Valentine's cards and other holiday merchandise.

In 2013, the Hindu extremist group Hindu Janajagruti Samiti claimed that Valentine's Day led to an increase in sexual violence and rape. As evidence, the group cited the increased sale of contraceptives near February 14. Sexual violence is a huge issue in

India, where women and girls have few rights and where law and tradition make it difficult to penalize men who attack women.

Despite all this opposition to Valentine's Day, ever-increasing numbers of India's young people are expressing their love with cards, gifts, flowers and dining out on February 14. Indeed, on Valentine's Day 2008, increased security was added to New Delhi University's rose garden to prevent the blooms from being picked by ardent lovers.

Valentine's Day in Africa

Egypt
Sometime in the 1950s, Ali Amin, an Egyptian journalist, ran a poll in his newspaper column about what the best date was to celebrate Valentine's Day. The majority of respondents chose November 4. Since then, this is the date for the holiday in that country. February 14 is also an occasion owing to Western influence and is referred to as "Heart's Day."

Ghana
The Happy FM radio station in Accra, Ghana, has sponsored a mass wedding ceremony on Valentine's Day since 2005. To date, over 400 couples have tied the knot at these ceremonies.

South Africa
In South Africa, women wear the name of their sweetheart on their sleeve on Valentine's Day. The man may be someone she is in a relationship with or just someone she fancies. Men try to catch a glimpse to see if the name is theirs.

For 10 years now, Robben Island off the coast of Cape Town has been the site of a Valentine's Day mass wedding. The island is the former prison where Nelson Mandela, anti-apartheid activist and former president of South Africa (1994–1999), spent several years as an inmate. In 1999, the United Nations declared it a World Heritage Site.

A Day of Love and Friendship: Latin America

Not everywhere is Valentine's Day reserved for lovers. In much of Latin America, Valentine's Day is called *Día del Amor y la Amistad* ("Day of Love and Friendship") and is a time to celebrate loving relationships of all kinds, with friends and family and even co-workers.

Passionate in Peru

♥ Men in Peru tend to give their wife or girlfriend orchids rather than roses. The country is home to over 3000 varieties of orchids. Stuffed animals are also a popular present.

♥ 2012 was the first year that Valentine's Day was a public holiday in Peru. February 13 was also made a holiday. Why? Because the Peruvian government loves money. Long weekends are great generators of income because they allow people just enough time to vacation around the country but not enough time to travel elsewhere.

♥ The Parque de Amor (Love Park) in Lima overlooks the Pacific Ocean and has a large statue of a couple kissing passionately. Sculpted by Victor Delfin, it is appropriately named "The Kiss." Brightly tiled walls with literary love quotes surround the kissing couple. The park opened on February 14, 1993, and has been a popular place for people to spend Valentine's Day ever since. Each year, couples compete in a friendly contest to see who can kiss the longest.

💜 Since Valentine's Day often coincides with Carnaval, it is a popular time for mass weddings in Peru. Twenty-four couples exchanged vows together on a beach in Peru on Valentine's Day 2013. Following the ceremony, the couples were treated to a boat ride along the coast. Three couples celebrated by jumping into the ocean. In 2012 and 2013, mass weddings were held in a swimming pool in Comas, Peru. In 2012, 200 couples exchanged vows in the refreshingly cool water.

💜 Valentine's Day 2010 saw five gay couples take part in fake wedding ceremonies in Lima's Love Park. The couples were protesting the fact that gay marriage was illegal in Peru (and still is). On Valentine's Day 2011, police in Lima broke up a kiss-in by gay and lesbian activists.

💜 The Peruvian city of Trujillo was founded by the Spaniards in 1535. On Valentine's Day 1619, a devastating earthquake shook the city, destroying many of the buildings and killing 400 people. Since then, the city has adopted St. Valentine as a protective patron saint.

Caring in Colombia

Colombia celebrates Día del Amor y la Amistad on the third
Saturday in September rather than February 14. The fun, however, begins in the weeks before Día del Amor y la Amistad,
when people draw for their *amigo secreto* ("secret friend"). Each
person anonymously gives a gift of an agreed upon value to their
secret friend sometime before the third Saturday of the month.
People also give their secret friend clues to their identity along
with other small gifts, like a candy or a joke. Colombian school
children usually have a party on the Friday before the big day.
Día del Amor y la Amistad is a day spent with loved ones. Gifts
are often exchanged, and people participate in activities that they
enjoy doing together.

Bolivian Love

In Bolivia, there are actually two days of love, neither of which
falls in February. On July 23, Bolivians celebrate Friendship
Day. They exchange cards and gifts and visit with their friends.
Then, on September 21, it is the Day of Love, Students' Day and
also the first day of spring. Lovers shower each other with gifts
and affection. School-age children might be given a gift or a special meal. Parties and awards ceremonies are held in schools.

Mexico and Guatemala

In Mexico, Día del Amor y la Amistad extends beyond lovers to
include all loving connections between people.

In Guatemala, Valentine's Day is called *Día del Cariño* ("Day of
Affection"). The fond feelings expressed on this day extend
beyond lovers to include family, friends, and colleagues.

Not Just for Latin America

In Finland and Estonia, Valentine's Day is known as Friend's
Day (*Ystävänpäivä* in Finnish; *Sõbrapäev* in Estonian). People

exchange cards and gifts with their friends. These exchanges include boyfriends and girlfriends, of course, and the day is a popular one for both weddings and engagements.

DID YOU KNOW?

In Cuba, Valentine's Day is known as Loving Day.

A Day of Lust: the Islamic World

Valentine's Day is a holiday that originated in the Christian world of Western Europe. With colonization and later globalization, the celebration of Valentine's Day has spread around the world. Some cultures have embraced this Western day of love with open arms, some more tentatively. Others have rejected it altogether.

The celebration of St. Valentine's Day is forbidden or strongly condemned in many Islamic countries, including Saudi Arabia, Pakistan, Iran and Indonesia.

Saudi Arabia Bans Valentine's Day

In Saudi Arabia, Valentine's Day is banned both because it is a Christian/Western celebration and because it encourages relations between non-married men and women. Saudi Arabia's religious police arrest all non-married couples caught celebrating Valentine's Day. They claim they are saving/guarding the virtue of the women from the false, sinful intentions of their male suitors.

During the week before Valentine's Day, agents of the Commission for the Promotion of Virtue and Prevention of Vice issue warnings. Beginning on February 13, they seize items associated with the holiday from stores. The sale of red roses and all

191

red merchandise is specifically banned. The black market for such items is huge.

Protests in Indonesia

Valentine's Day is not banned in Indonesia, but many segments of the population strongly oppose it. Protests and declarations against Valentine's Day occur every year. Indonesian Muslim women protested the incursion of Valentine's Day into their country at a rally in Malang, East Java, on February 14, 2012. The banners they carried listed the many reasons why the protestors were opposed to Valentine's Day. They saw Valentine's Day as promoting casual sex and promiscuity, alcohol consumption and Western culture. A year later, schoolgirls in the city marched in an anti-Valentine's Day protest. They held placards that proclaimed the day Headscarf Day and distributed pamphlets encouraging women to cover their bodies from head to toe.

The Indonesia Ulema Council, the country's top Islamic body, stated in 2011 that they no longer worried that Valentine's Day would lead to an outbreak of premarital sexual activity among the nation's teenagers. They now believe it is a day of relatively harmless but foolish expressions of love, a fad that they feel will pass with time. A spokesman for Indonesia's largest Muslim organization, Nahdlatul Ulama, said that Valentine's Day was for adults, not for teenagers. Officers for public order in Indonesia patrolled the streets and raided hotels on Valentine's Day 2012 in an effort to prevent unmarried couples from engaging in sexual activity.

Some people in the island nation, including Muslims, celebrate Valentine's Day nonetheless. Expressions of affection are usually kept low key because public displays of affection are generally frowned upon by Muslims.

Policing Valentine's Day in Malaysia

In Malaysia, a country where two-thirds of the population is Muslim, the government's Department of Islamic Development ran an anti-Valentine's Day campaign in 2011 called Mind the Valentine's Day Trap. It stated that Valentine's Day was a non-Islamic holiday that promoted vice.

In Malaysia, it is illegal for unmarried Muslim couples to be alone together in a private place. So when police raided a hotel on Valentine's Day 2010, only the unmarried Muslim couples were charged with having premarital sex and issued fines of up to $1000 and six months in jail.

Passionate Opinions in Pakistan

Valentine's Day is a highly contested holiday in Pakistan as it is in many areas of the Muslim world. Some people ignore the festivities, others embrace them and still others do their utmost to stop them. Religious extremists, led by the fundamentalist

Islamic group Jamaat-e-Islami, condemn Valentine's Day as un-Islamic. They say that marriages in their country are arranged and are a matter of duty to one's family; they are not love matches as in the West.

For years now, contrasting opinions about Valentine's Day have been seen on the streets of Pakistan's major cities around the middle of February. On February 14, 2013, billboards appeared in the city of Karachi displaying a black heart along with the message that Valentine's Day is an insensitive and anti-Islamic holiday. The billboards were posted by Jamaat-e-Islami. In Peshwar, extremists burned Valentine's Day cards and called for a day of modesty. However, many stores still did a brisk business in holiday-related items. Authorities asked television and radio stations to be circumspect in regards to any Valentine's Day content in their programming so as not to offend anyone too greatly.

Slaves to Love in Uzbekistan

The government of Uzbekistan has banned the celebration of all Western holidays, including Valentine's Day. Officials in Uzbekistan are promoting the celebration of the anniversary of the birth of the Mughal emperor Babur on February 14 rather than Valentine's Day, a corrupting Western celebration that has been gaining in popularity there over the past decade. Babur was born in the Uzbek town of Andijan. He created a large empire in Southeast Asia in the 16th century. An Uzbek government official reportedly stated that Valentine's Day makes people slaves to their sexual urges, making them easier for rebels and terrorists to control.

DID YOU KNOW?

The government of Turkmenistan banned the celebration of Valentine's Day because it is not a traditional Turkmen holiday.

United Arab Emirates

Although a largely Muslim country, the United Arab Emirates
has not banned Valentine's Day like a number of its neighbors,
recognizing it as good for the economy. The city of Dubai has
become a place where people of many cultures and nationalities
reside, each with their own ideas of acceptable behavior. To
avoid the problem of public displays of affection frowned upon
by many citizens, several high schools either reduced their hours
or closed entirely on Valentine's Day 2013.

DID YOU  KNOW?

Like the U.A.E., the Muslim country of Iraq allows the celebration of Valentine's Day because it is good for the economy.

Alternate Days of Love

January 25—St. Dwynwen's Day—Wales

Dwynwen was a Welsh princess who lived in the fifth century.
She fell madly in love with a young man named Maelon.
Unfortunately, King Brychan Brycheinog, Dwynwen's father,
disapproved of the match and made arrangements for his daughter to marry someone else. Distraught, Dwynwen fled into the
forest. There, an angel came to her and gave her a potion
designed to quite literally cool the ardor of the lovers. The potion
worked too well, and, after drinking it, Maelon turned to ice.
Dwynwen prayed for help. The angel heard her prayer and
granted Dwynwen three wishes. First, the princess asked to have
Maelon restored to life. Second, she desired to never marry since
she could not marry the man she desired. Third, she asked that
God watch over those in love and help them to be together.

Dwynwen became a nun and lived the rest of her life in a convent on Llanddwyn Island, the remains of which can still be seen today. The site was a popular pilgrimage destination in the Middle Ages. Pilgrims would visit a well located there and observe the movements of the fish living in it. These movements were said to reveal the fate of those in love.

In the 1960s, the observance of St. Dwynwen's Day was revived by Vera Williams. The college student designed four romantic cards for lovers to exchange on St. Dwynwen's Day. The custom caught on, and 50 years later it is still going strong.

February 18—Sepandārmazgān—Iran

The Iranian government is promoting the revival of the ancient Zoroastrian holiday of Sepandārmazgān to combat the incursion of the Western holiday of Valentine's Day, which is deemed to be an immoral celebration of lust. Sepandārmazgān, in contrast, is a day on which husbands honor their wives' obedient and dutiful behavior. It is celebrated on February 18.

February 24—Dragobete's Day—Romania

In Romania, February 24 is known as Dragobete's Day. Dragobete was the son of Baba Dochia, an ancient character associated with the return of spring. Dragobete was an ancient Romanian fertility god, similar in many ways to Cupid of the Romans or Eros of the Greeks. The day is for lovers, and men might give a bouquet of spring flowers to their sweethearts. It is important for couples to kiss a lot and not to argue in order to bring good fortune to their relationship in the coming year. Any man who hurts a woman on Dragobete's Day will suffer bad luck all year. If a couple dances together on Dragobete's Day and one of them steps over the foot of the other, that person will be the dominant person in the relationship. Single women must make sure to see a man on this day to ensure that they will not remain single. It is also the day on which birds are said to choose their mates.

March 8—Women's Day—Poland
Prior to the collapse of Communism, Valentine's Day was not a holiday celebrated in Poland. Dzien Kobiet (Women's Day) was and is observed on March 8. On this day, all women are honored with gifts (often flowers) and displays of love and respect. Poles now also celebrate Valentine's Day.

April 15—All Lovers' Day—Kazakhstan
In 2001, the government of Kazakhstan created a Kazakh alternative to Valentine's Day. Called All Lovers' Day, the date was set for April 15, when the weather begins to warm up. The celebrations include the release of paper lanterns into the air at dusk, thereby releasing all one's problems. The holiday has been slow to catch on.

All Lovers' Day revolves around Kozy Korpersh and Bayan Sulu, the lovers in a 13th-century epic. Bayan Sulu and Kozy Korpersh were in love and wanted to get married, but Bayan Sulu's father opposed the match; he wanted his daughter to marry Kodar, a wealthier man than Kozy Korpersh. The lovers decided to run away and elope. As they were making their escape, Kodar shot and killed Kozy Korpersh with an arrow. Enraged, Bayan Sulu sought out Kodar and killed him in retaliation. She then returned to the body of her dead lover and committed suicide. The mausoleum where the bodies of the two ill-fated lovers are said to lie still stands in Kazakhstan today.

April 23—St. George's Day—Catalonia

In Catalonia, St. George's Day on April 23 is a day for expressing love and affection through the exchange of gifts. Historically, people gave roses to loved ones on this day. Then in 1923, a bookseller noticed that two great writers, Miguel Cervantes and William Shakespeare, died on this day in 1616, and he decided to use that fact as a way to promote the sale of books instead of roses as gifts for men. The idea was a huge success that now results in the sale of 800,000 books annually.

Roses remain the gift of choice for women, with the color of the flower revealing the exact nature of the sentiment conveyed. A man gives a red rose to his sweetheart. Friends exchange blue roses as a symbol of trust. A pink rose is a sign of gratitude.

May 1—Czech Republic

Valentine's Day first appeared in the Czech Republic following the Velvet Revolution and the fall of Communism in 1989. While it has been promoted by businesses, it has never really caught on. This is because the Czechs already have a day of love—May 1, when couples kiss under blossoming cherry trees to ensure health and happiness for the coming year.

June 13—St. Anthony's Day—Brazil

Valentine's Day is not celebrated in Brazil. Instead, Brazilians celebrate *Dia dos Namorados* ("Day of Love") on the feast day of St. Anthony, patron saint of marriage. Couples exchange presents. Some single women take pieces of paper and write on each one the name of a guy they like. They crumple these up and then go to bed. The next morning on Dia dos Namorados, they select a paper from the pile. The name on the paper will be their future husband.

July 1–7—Sweetness Week and Friendship Day—Argentina

In Argentina, love and friendship are allocated a whole week of celebration. From July 1 to 7, Argentines give friends and family gifts of hugs, kisses and candy as part of Sweetness Week. The festivities culminate on July 7, known as Friendship Day.

July 8—Day of Married Love and Family Happiness—Russia

The Day of Married Love and Family Happiness is a new holiday in Russia. It was created by the Russian government in 2008 to counter the Western holiday of Valentine's Day. The date was chosen to honor the married Russian Orthodox saints Peter and Febronia.

Peter was a prince of Murom. Febronia was a Russian holy woman, born of peasant parents. When Peter fell very ill,

Febronia was brought to the palace to pray for his safe recovery.
Peter did recover, and the couple fell in love. They married
against the wishes of Peter's aristocratic family. The couple are
said to have had a chaste marriage, later entering into monastic
life. They died on the same day and are buried together.

DID YOU  KNOW?

The Russian city of Belgorod has forbidden all government-
funded institutions, including schools, from participating in
Valentine's Day festivities. Officials declared that the Western
holiday promotes promiscuity rather than love.

Tu B'Av

Tu B'Av is the traditional Jewish day for love. It is celebrated on
the 15th day of the Jewish month of Av. On this day, Jewish
men demonstrate their love and affection to their sweethearts.
Giving cards and bouquets of flowers is popular just as on
Valentine's Day. Marriage proposals and weddings are common.

The origins of the festival have been lost in the mists of time,
but the most likely explanation is that Tu B'Av was the day when
some sort of ban against intermarriages between the tribes of
Israel was lifted. The earliest record of this festival dates back to
the second century. In ancient times, Jewish girls would dress up
in pretty white dresses and go to meet the boys in the vineyards;
it was an opportunity for courting. The festival, however, was
only a minor one in the Jewish calendar, and over the centuries
it fell out of use. It was only after the creation of the modern
state of Israel in the 20th century that the festival was revived.

LONELY HEARTS AND LUSTFUL TEMPTATIONS: ANTI-VALENTINE'S SENTIMENTS

The Valentine's Day Blues

Valentine's Day is not a happy day for everyone. For those without a partner to share the day, it can be a depressing time. Seeing happy couples everywhere can highlight a single person's feelings of loneliness. Klaus Nomi's song "Valentine's Day" is about how awful and lonely and depressing it feels to be single on Valentine's Day, having to watch other people revel in their love for one another. The song was released in 2007 as part of a compilation of songs.

Some single people take a proactive approach to this day of love by doing something nice for themselves. Up to 15 percent of American women send themselves flowers on Valentine's Day, while in Japan, men can purchase Valentine's Day insurance. This insurance guarantees that the man will receive chocolates (the traditional gift for men on Valentine's Day in Japan).

Anti-Valentine's Day parties are becoming increasingly popular. Some are public events hosted by a nightclub or bar. Others are private affairs. These events allow those without a partner to have fun on Valentine's Day and at the same time vent some of the negative feelings this holiday can bring out. For example, Las Vegas' Tao Asian Bistro and Nightclub hosts an anti-Valentine's Day party called Cupid Is Stupid. Attendees are invited to bring a photo of their ex and pin it to the huge dartboard.

Sadly, in some cases, the feelings of loneliness and rejection can be extreme at this time of year. It is no surprise that the rates of suicides, attempted suicides and calls to suicide hotlines all spike around Valentine's Day. During the 1980s, a number of suicide pacts by teenagers in the U.S. occurred on Valentine's Day. In 2005, members of an internet chat room for people interested in the subject of suicide were encouraged by Gerald Krien of Glamath Falls, Oregon, to join together in a mass suicide on Valentine's Day. Krien was arrested and charged with trying to solicit aggravated murder.

Singles Awareness Day
There is a movement to create a holiday on February 14 called Singles Awareness Day (or S.A.D.) that celebrates the single life. S.A.D. festivities range from fun-filled group events for single people celebrating life to supportive gatherings for those who feel left out or inferior on a day that celebrates couples.

Joseph Vincent wrote a song entitled "S.A.D. (Singles Awareness Day)" in 2012 in which he speaks of the heartache many without a partner feel on Valentine's Day.

Quirkyalone Day

♥ Quirkyalone Day was established as another alternative to the highly commercialized Valentine's Day. It is also celebrated on February 14.

♥ Magazine publisher Sasha Cagen is behind the idea for Quirkyalone Day.

♥ Quirkyalone Day stresses individuality, but it is not limited to single people.

♥ Quirkyalone Day celebrates all types of love, for partners, family, friends and for oneself. It also reminds people to value themselves as individuals within each of these types of relationships.

♥ Quirkyalone Day was first celebrated in 2003 in Glasgow, Scotland, and three American cities: San Francisco, Providence and New York City.

♥ By 2005, the holiday was being celebrated on four continents—North America, Europe, Asia and Australia.

♥ There are even awards called Quirkys for best movie, book, etc., that captures the Quirkyalone spirit of uniqueness and individuality of people and relationships.

♥ Some card manufacturers are now producing Quirkyalone cards.

Unhappy Valentine's Day

Not everyone who is in a relationship has a wonderful, romantic time on Valentine's Day. Some people forget what day it is. Some people expect more out of the day than their partner does. Retailers and the media have turned it into a day where gift-giving is no longer seen as voluntary, but as an obligation and an expectation. When the desires and expectations of one partner are out of sync with those of the other, the day is likely to end unhappily. For the following couples, things went worse than for most.

Unfulfilled Expectations

Twenty-two-year-old Kierra Reed did not take it well when her boyfriend Henry Brown forgot to buy her a Valentine's Day present in 2012. Instead of crying or giving Brown the cold shoulder, Reed attacked him. Brown locked himself in a bedroom to escape Reed, who then grabbed a knife and began to stab the door, threatening to cut and even kill Brown. Cincinnati police soon arrested Reed, charging her with aggravated menacing.

An Unexpected Gift

Stacey Schoeck of Atlanta, Georgia, chose Valentine's Day 2010 as the day she would have her husband Richard murdered. Stacey arranged to have a hit-man shoot Richard when the couple met in a park that evening to exchange Valentine's Day gifts. She pled guilty to paying personal trainer Reginald Coleman $10,000 to kill her fifth husband. She allegedly arranged the hit to collect her husband's life insurance money. Instead of spending money, she's spending life in prison.

Bloody Valentine

Mentally ill meth addict Tiffany Sutton, 23, seduced Robert McDaniel, 43, with offers of kinky sex for Valentine's Day 2007.

The two people had known each other for only two days when they spent some time together drinking and doing drugs. One thing led to another, and McDaniel found himself tied to the bed anticipating a hot night. Instead, Sutton came at him with a knife and stabbed him seven times and slashed him a further two times, telling the horrified man that she liked to drink blood. McDaniel eventually managed to free himself while the crazed woman drank the blood flowing from a wound on his leg. He ran to the washroom and locked himself in before passing out. A friend later found him there. Tempe, Arizona, police arrested Sutton on charges of aggravated assault.

An Explosive Love
David McCoy of Alliance, Ohio, did not take rejection well. The 32-year-old man was arrested by police after he made a bomb and attached it to the undercarriage of the truck owned by his estranged wife's new boyfriend in the hopes of blowing the couple up on Valentine's Day 2013. Luckily, the boyfriend noticed the bomb, which was gift-wrapped in red tissue paper, and contacted the authorities, who removed it safely. McCoy was charged with attempted murder and illegally manufacturing explosives.

Digital Dumping

In 2013, a Manchester woman named Laura picked a very public way to dump her boyfriend—and on Valentine's Day of all days. Laura paid to have an announcement to her boyfriend Dan displayed on a digital billboard screen at the Esso garage he frequented. The display read, "Dan, I'm leaving you for Gary. Your clothes are at your mum's & I've changed the locks. Sorry to do this on Valentine's Day. Laura." Wow!

Who Will Say I Do?

In 2009, the couple that had booked a Valentine's Day wedding package at the Best Western Hotel in Brighton, England, broke up just weeks before the nuptials. The hotel decided that rather than letting such a romantic day go to waste, they would auction the package on eBay.

Museum of Broken Relationships

When Drazen Grubisic and Olinka Vistica divorced, they could not decide what to do with all their joint sentimental possessions. What they did in the end was unique: they decided to open the Museum of Broken Relationships. Located in Zagreb, Croatia, the museum houses donations from all over the world. People who have gone through a breakup can donate an item of significance along with an anonymous note that includes the date and location of the relationship. The museum, which opened in 2010, contains a dizzying variety of memorabilia arranged on tables designed to look like a shattered heart.

The Museum of Broken Relationships aims to give donors "a chance to overcome an emotional collapse through creation, by contributing to the museum's collection." The owners say that the number of visitors to the museum doubles around Valentine's Day.

♥ There is an ax that a Berlin woman used to destroy all the furniture that belonged to her ex ("The more the room filled with chopped furniture, [the more] I felt better.").

♥ A garter belt was accompanied by the note, "I never put them on. The relationship might have lasted longer if I had."

♥ A cork from a woman in England who caught her fiancé cheating on her came from the bottle of champagne she drank to celebrate her lucky escape.

♥ "Darling, should you ever get the ridiculous idea to walk into a cultural institution like a museum for the first time in your life, you'll remember me." This note came with a blue frisbee.

♥ A Turkish woman donated a bottle of nasal spray: "He bought this to stop his snoring. I could not go to sleep because of his snoring. Now I can't go to sleep because of the pain of heartbreak."

♥ "He gave me his cellphone so I couldn't call him anymore."

♥ A teddy bear holding a heart with the words "I Love You" was sent in with the note, "'I love you'—WHAT A LIE! LIES, DAMN LIES! Yes, it's like that when you are young, naïve and in love. And you don't realize your boyfriend started dating you just because he wanted to take you to bed! I got this teddy bear for Valentine's. He survived on top of my closet in a plastic bag, because it wasn't him who hurt me, but the idiot who left him behind."

I Love You Not: Valentine's Day and Divorce

♥ Divorce rates jump 30–40 percent in the weeks after Valentine's Day.

💜 Manchester radio station Key 103 held a contest on Valentine's Day 2000. The prize was a free divorce. Couples went on air to list their grievances against each other. The winners, Darren Wilson and Kath Rose, won not only a free divorce but also a free vacation with their new partners to a destination of their choosing. Both chose Mexico!

💜 On the eve of Valentine's Day 2012, the British company QuickDivorceUK.com launched its new service. Couples can fly to the Dominican Republic and get divorced by a judge there the very next day. Happy Valentine's Day!

💜 For Valentine's Day 2012, a controversial radio station in New Zealand known as The Rock created a stir in that country by advertising that a woman named Sam would call her unsuspecting husband and tell him on the air that she wanted a divorce. The station agreed to pay for the divorce. The stunt backfired when Sam turned out to be a lesbian (same-sex marriages were illegal in New Zealand at the time) who had volunteered to make the call to protest what the couple viewed as the radio station's immoral and unethical bid for publicity.

💜 A British woman who filed for divorce in 2012 cited her husband's repeated failure to remember Valentine's Day as one of the reasons she was seeking a divorce. Her husband agreed to plead no contest to her accusations of "unreasonable behavior."

💜 To celebrate Valentine's Day 2013, attorney Walter Bentley III of Southfield, Michigan, held a contest to give one couple a free divorce.

💜 Albert Einstein and first wife, Mileva Maric, divorced on February 14, 1919.

♥ On Valentine's Day 1989, Robin Givens was granted a divorce from boxer Mike Tyson. After years of being physically abused, it must have been a truly happy Valentine's Day for Givens.

♥ Actor Michael Welch (*Twilight* series) and his wife, Marissa Lefton, filed jointly for divorce on Valentine's Day 2013.

Broken-hearted Booze

Maybe this Valentine's Day is not the happiest one for you, and you are spending it alone. Well, if you are looking for some liquid company to share the day with, here are some anti-Valentine's Day suggestions.

♥ For the divorced person's thirst buds, there's Alimony Ale (6.8 percent) from California's Buffalo Bill Brewery.

♥ Still feeling a bit angry about a recent breakup? How about a bottle of His Fault (white) or Her Fault (red) California red wine?

♥ This Valentine's Day you can spend time with a Fat Bastard wine, which will likely provide much better company than your ex of the same name. There are six Fat Bastards from which to choose: shiraz, merlot, chardonnay, pinot noir, sauvignon blanc and cabernet sauvignon.

♥ If the Fat Bastard wine does not quite fit the bill for you, there are several beer options: Weyerbacher Brewing Company produces Blithering Idiot English barleywine; Portneuf Valley Brewing offers Belligerent Ass nut brown ale; Arrogant Bastard Ale is courtesy of Stone Brewing Company; and Bitter Bitch imperial beer is made by Astoria Brewing Company.

School Days

North American school children have traditionally celebrated
Valentine's Day by giving cards and sometimes even candy treats
to their classmates. Indeed, this practice kept Valentine's Day
alive and well in the U.S. in the early 20th century when it all
but died out in Britain. In the past, students only gave cards to
their friends and perhaps someone they had a secret crush on.
These cards were either placed in a mailbox on the teacher's desk
to be distributed later by the teacher, or placed in individual
mailbags (usually a decorated paper bag) attached to each child's
desk. This practice resulted in some children getting lots of
Valentines while others got only a few or even none at all. Today,
most schools require each student to bring a Valentine's card for
each of their classmates. Increasingly, treats are not allowed
because of food allergies. Some schools are banning the celebration of Valentine's Day altogether for various reasons.

♥ In 1998, public elementary schools in Hillsborough, New Jersey, banned the celebration of Valentine's Day. The day, which is named for a saint, was deemed too religious! School officials replaced the annual festivities with Special Person Day, which was essentially the same thing but with a more politically correct name. Since then, many of the schools in the district have reverted to celebrating Valentine's Day.

♥ In 2001, Morgan Nyman, a second-grader at Cushing Elementary School in Wisconsin was not allowed to hand out her Valentine's cards to her classmates because they had religious messages printed on them, such as "Jesus Loves You." The Liberty Counsel filed a lawsuit against the school on behalf of the Nyman family. A new school policy was implemented by the local school district as a result, which allows Valentine's cards (and other materials) to be distributed that contain religious messages so long as they do not seek to convert or indoctrinate other students.

♥ In 2010, Peter Turner, headmaster of Ashcombe Primary School in Weston-super-Mare, Somerset, banned the exchange of Valentine's cards at his school. He said that such declarations of love were too confusing for the students, who were still developing emotionally.

♥ Walkersville Elementary School in Walkersville, Maryland, banned Valentine's Day at the school in 2011. In 2012, Valentine's Day festivities were back, with some restrictions, after parents complained. Children are now allowed to give out cards to their classmates as long as no food or candy is exchanged, and the students must give a card to every student in the class.

♥ In 2013, Lake Nona and Cypress Creek high schools in Florida banned large Valentine's Day gift exchanges at school, saying that the exchanges and deliveries were too disruptive and that the schools wanted to maintain their focus on academics.

♥ Salemwood Elementary School in Malden, Massachusetts, will no longer be celebrating Valentine's Day. Beginning in 2013, the holiday was banned at the school and replaced with Friendship Week, to be celebrated in mid-February. The school made the decision because of the numerous cultures represented by the school's students and a desire to have a festivity that everyone could participate in. Students were asked to bring friendship cards to exchange with each other. The decision created an uproar among the parents in the community.

DID YOU KNOW?

In the 1980s, Mattel introduced the Happy Holidays series of Barbie dolls. Every year, a new Valentine's Day Barbie was produced.

On-screen Heartache

Valentine Horror
The 2001 movie simply entitled *Valentine* tells the story of two very unhappy Valentine's Days indeed. The story begins in 1988 at a junior high school. The Valentine's Day dance is approaching, and student Jeremy Melton asks four girls to go with him. Three of the girls (Shelley, Lily and Paige) cruelly turn him down, while the fourth (Kate) declines nicely. Jeremy, a social outcast, ends up making out with another girl under the bleachers until they are spotted by several of the more popular male students. The girl, Dorothy, claims Jeremy was assaulting her,

and after being beat up by the other boys, Jeremy is sent to reform school.

Years later, the women who cruelly rejected Jeremy in junior high school receive taunting Valentines from an unknown person. Dorothy's reads, "Roses are red, Violets are blue, They'll need dental records to identify you." Lily gets a box of maggot-filled chocolates. The women prepare for Valentine's Day and a costume party being hosted by Dorothy. By the end of the movie, three of the women have been horrifically murdered. The killer is discovered...or is he?

We Love You, Charlie Brown!

Be My Valentine, Charlie Brown first aired in 1975. The television special tells the story of Linus and Charlie's disappointing Valentine's Day. Like children across North America, those at the boys' school exchange Valentine's cards. Charlie is hoping to get a lot of cards and takes a briefcase to school to carry them all home. Unfortunately, as many children can attest, not everyone gets Valentines at these school festivities. Charlie Brown receives only a candy heart that says "Forget it, Kid" and goes home sad. The next day, Violet, a girl from school, brings him a used Valentine to apologize for her own lack of thoughtfulness. Ever the optimist, Charlie hopes this means things will go better next year.

Linus, on the other hand, is smitten with his teacher and buys her a big heart-shaped box of chocolates, only to discover that she already has a boyfriend. He throws away the chocolates in frustration, not realizing that Sally had hoped the chocolates were for her. Both Sally and Linus experience heartbreak on Valentine's Day.

Charles Schultz's portrayal of Valentine's Day has become a classic, airing each year. It touches a chord in everyone with its realism. Valentine's Day is not about love and romance for everyone. For some, it is a day of heartache, heartbreak and loneliness. However, Charlie Brown encourages everyone to think positively: maybe Valentine's Day next year will be better.

A Charlie Brown Valentine first aired on ABC in 2002. It is another tale of unrequited love. Charlie Brown pines for a little red-headed girl who does not even know he exists. At the same time, Marcie and Peppermint Patty compete for Chuck's attention. No one succeeds in capturing the heart of their beloved.

DID YOU KNOW?

When *Be My Valentine, Charlie Brown* first aired in 1975, hundreds of children sent Valentines to Charlie Brown at the CBS studio.

A Valentine's Day Tragedy

On February 12, 1884, Theodore Roosevelt (1858–1919) must have felt like he was the happiest man alive. His beloved wife Ann had just given birth to their first child, a healthy baby girl whom they named Alice. Roosevelt was not home for the birth, which he had been convinced would occur on Valentine's Day. He received the happy news via telegram while in Albany at the State Assembly and quickly packed up and headed home to his wife and newborn daughter.

Roosevelt had met his wife Ann five years earlier and was quickly smitten by her. In his diary, he wrote on the day they met, "As long as I live, I shall never forget how sweetly she looked, and how prettily she greeted me." Seven months later, Roosevelt proposed. Ann, however, took her time—eight months—to accept! The happy couple announced their engagement to family and friends on Valentine's Day 1880 and were married that fall on Roosevelt's birthday, October 27.

When Roosevelt arrived home from Albany the next day, he found both his wife and mother gravely ill. Roosevelt's mother, Martha, had been sick for several days, but his wife had only become ill after giving birth. Roosevelt rushed to his wife's bedside and remained there, holding and comforting her into the wee hours of the morning, when he was summoned to his mother's room. There, on February 14 at 3:00 AM, Martha Bulloch Roosevelt (1835–1884) passed away from typhoid fever.

After shedding tears of grief for his departed mother, Roosevelt returned to be with his wife. Ann, however, showed no signs of recovery. In fact, she appeared to be worsening. Roosevelt held her in his arms for several hours before she slipped away only 36 hours after giving birth to their daughter.

It is unclear what caused the death of Ann Hathaway Lee Roosevelt (1861–1884). It is thought to have been either a type of kidney disease known at the time as Bright's disease, or complications resulting from childbirth, such as toxemia or pre-eclampsia. It may have even been a combination of these conditions. Whatever the cause, Ann was gone and so was Martha. Roosevelt was crushed. His diary entry from that night of February 14, 1884, reads simply, "The light has gone out of my life."

Roosevelt rarely ever spoke of his first wife after that night. Ironically, their daughter Alice (1884–1980) gave birth to her only daughter, Paulina Longworth (1925–1957) on Valentine's Day 1925.

DID YOU  KNOW?

Theodore Roosevelt is the man for whom teddy bears, a popular Valentine's Day gift, were named.

The St. Valentine's Day Massacre

Jack "Machine Gun" McGurn (born Vincenzo Gibaldi) was mob boss Al Capone's right hand man. Born and raised in Chicago, McGurn's early years had been good ones. The death of his father when he was a teenager set McGurn's life on the path that ultimately led to his violent death. Like many people during the Prohibition years, McGurn's father had taken to selling a bit of moonshine on the side to make some extra money. Chicago was a place where small-time moonshine operators needed gang approval to operate. McGurn's father tried to operate independently and paid with his life. Jack is said to have vowed to get revenge for his father's death.

McGurn took up boxing and shooting, becoming an ace shot. In a few years, he was working for Capone's gang. His many kills made him a favorite with Capone, who rarely went anywhere without him. McGurn's trademark was leaving a nickel in the hand of his victim, a show of contempt meaning the man was a lowlife, a "nickel and dimer."

McGurn is believed by many people to have been a key player in the St. Valentine's Day Massacre. On February 14, 1929, seven men were gunned down in a warehouse at 2122 North Clark Street. Six of the men (Frank and Peter Gusenberg, Albert Kachellek, Adam Heyer, Albert Weinshank and John May) were known members of the Moran gang, Capone's main competitor. The seventh victim, Reinhardt Schwimmer, was a known associate. The men had been lured to the location, probably with promises of a big shipment of booze. Four other gang members, including George "Bugs" Moran himself, were late getting to the meeting. Seeing a police car in front of the warehouse, they changed their plans and saved their lives. Witnesses saw four men, two dressed as cops and two wearing suits and coats, enter the building before the firing started. The seven men were shot down by bullets from Thompson machine guns, McGurn's weapon of choice.

The identity of the shooters has never been established, but the massacre shocked the city of Chicago. McGurn continued to work closely with Al Capone until the boss' imprisonment for income tax evasion a few years later. Things began to go downhill for McGurn after that. Other gang members, jealous of his close ties with Capone, distanced themselves from him. The Great Depression took its toll. McGurn began to sell drugs on the side to boost his income, an activity not condoned by the gang. He was gunned down in an alley by five men on

Valentine's Day 1936. He was only 34. In his hand was a nickel and beside his body lay a not-so-humorous Valentine's card:

> *You've lost your job,*
> *You've lost your dough,*
> *Your jewels and handsome houses.*
> *But things could be worse, you know,*
> *At least you have your trousers.*

Unlawful Loving

Lottery of Love

A former Valentine's Day custom in France was the lottery of love. Single young people living across the street from each other would pair up for the day. Those who did not fancy their partners could abandon them for another. Women left without a partner would make fires and burn drawings of the men who spurned them while shouting abuse at them. Then, in March 1776, the French government made these pairings illegal because of the hard feelings created by ill matches and spurned Valentines. Like most traditions, the lottery of love did not fade away quickly. Three years later, police were handing out 100 livre fines to people who insisted on continuing the practice. As late as July 1816, the police in Metz were still stopping people from celebrating Valentine's Day as they had in generations past.

A High Price to Pay for Love

In 1875, 22-year-old Huntingdonshire laborer and repeat offender William Coles was convicted of stealing a Valentine. He was sentenced to three months of hard labor. Let's hope his beloved was worth it!

Unseemly Behavior

The Puritans who moved from England to North America to
found communities based upon their own strict religious beliefs
frowned on the Old World custom of Valentine's Day, as well as
on public displays of affection. Some communities actually
banned celebrating Valentine's Day just as they banned the
observance of Christmas Day: "No lad shall attend a maid on
the fourteenth of February."

But after three long years at sea, Captain James Kemble had
apparently forgotten these restrictions. Arriving in his home port
of Boston on February 14, 1764, the captain ran to find his wife
on the streets of the city, where he took her in his arms and gave
her a long, Valentine's Day kiss. His wife, no doubt, appreciated
the sentiment, but city officials did not. The captain found himself promptly thrown in the stocks for two hours for his
unseemly behavior!

Bonds of Love

Police arrested Oregon couple Nikolas Harbar and Stephanie
Pelzner after a 2012 Valentine's Day role-playing act alarmed
witnesses. Pelzner, in the role of a kidnap victim, lay bound and
naked in the backseat of Harbar's car. Even though she assured
a concerned passerby that she was fine, the witness reported the
incident to Portland police, who issued a city-wide alert.
The arrested couple spent the remainder of Valentine's Day
behind bars.

Unexpected Deliveries

Police in Canyon City, Colorado, used Valentine's Day 2013 as
a cover to capture six people with outstanding arrest warrants.
Officers posed as floral delivery men and made the arrests when
pretending to deliver flowers to the wanted individuals. Talk
about a disappointing gift!

Kiss of Contempt

British couple Samson Paine (25) and Karla Shaw (24) shared
a passionate embrace after Paine was convicted of robbery and
assault causing bodily harm for the theft of some cigarettes and
money from a woman. The trial took place in Maidstone Crown
Court in Kent on February 14, 2013. The judge ordered the couple to stop kissing. When they blatantly ignored him, he charged
them both with contempt of court, saying he hoped it had been
worth it. To which Shaw replied that it had and wished the
judge a happy Valentine's Day.

Not Your Average Teddy Bears

In 2013, police in the U.S. made two separate discoveries of
Valentine's Day teddy bears being used to smuggle drugs. First,
in early February, cops in Ontario, Oregon, pulled over a vehicle
for failing to signal when turning. The routine stop quickly
revealed two Valentine's Day teddy bear gift baskets full of
$200,000 worth of hidden heroin. Sonla Marquez-Lozano, 22,

and Yedid Zamudio-Vazquez, 20, are facing charges of drug possession and distribution. It can be assumed that the two women did not have a happy Valentine's Day.

The second discovery was made across the country, when postal inspectors noticed a suspicious package addressed to Lawrence Ligocki. They contacted the Massachusetts State Police, who brought a police dog to the post office and identified the package as containing drugs. Immediately after accepting delivery of the seemingly innocent Valentine's Day teddy bear and heart-shaped box of chocolates, Ligocki, 63, was arrested. Inside the teddy bear, police found several packages of crystal methamphetamine. A search of the suspect's house turned up more of the drug.

Passion in Prison

Fani Moyo, a prisoner in Harare Central Prison in Zimbabwe, was thrilled when his secret girlfriend of seven months gave him a card for Valentine's Day 2013. Indeed, Moyo was so excited to receive the card that he bragged about it to several other inmates, some of whom reported it to prison officials. Prison guards searched Moyo's jail cell and found the Valentine's card. What's wrong with a prisoner getting a card on Valentine's Day? Nothing, except when the sender is a female prison guard. Patisiwe Mapuranga has been suspended from her job for having an inappropriate relationship with a prisoner. An investigation is currently underway.

Powder Among the Petals

In 2010, customs officials in Amsterdam discovered four kilograms of cocaine hidden among 20,000 roses being imported into the Netherlands from Colombia for Valentine's Day.

That incident was not the only time a shipment of flowers for Valentine's Day bouquets has been used to smuggle drugs. In 2012, English businessman Gary Pattison was caught smuggling cocaine in a shipment of chrysanthemums to his floral shop in Hull for Valentine's Day arrangements. Pattison was sentenced to 18 years in jail for the offense.

Cupid's Cautionary Notes

If you plan to spend Valentine's Day in any of these places in the U.S., you may want to be careful!

💜 Abilene, Texas—it is illegal for a man to whistle at a woman.

💜 Alabama—if you live in Alabama, you'd better plan ahead: it is illegal to buy a sex toy on Valentine's Day.

💜 Dyersburg, Tennessee—it is illegal for a woman to ask a man out on a date.

💜 Halethorpe, Maryland—it is illegal to kiss for more than one minute, so be sure to have other activities planned for this special day.

💜 Kalamazoo, Michigan—men, you cannot serenade your girlfriend here this Valentine's Day; ladies, depending on your boyfriend, this may not be such a bad thing.

💜 Minnesota—give a girl a hug, a kiss or a box of chocolates in front of her parents, and it is equivalent to a marriage proposal!

💜 Nebraska—planning on a fun-filled evening in a hotel this Valentine's Day? Remember, you will have to wear a cotton nightshirt supplied by the hotel during all your bedroom activities. Sexy enough for you? Oh yeah!

💜 Ottumwa, Iowa—no man may wink at a female stranger. Guys, introduce yourself first, then wink all you want.

♥ Riverside, California—a health ordinance states that two people intending to kiss must first wash their lips with carbonated rose water.

♥ San Antonio, Texas—it is illegal to flirt in this city.

♥ Washington D.C.—if sex is on your mind this Valentine's Day, be prepared to get busy in that old standby, the missionary position. Any other position is against the law.

♥ Willowdale, Oregon—men, you can whisper sweet words of love to your partner during sex, but absolutely no talking dirty; it is prohibited by law.

ABOUT THE AUTHOR

Tonya Lambert is an author and historian who currently divides her time between Saskatoon, Saskatchewan, and Edmonton, Alberta. She holds an MA in history from the University of Saskatchewan. Tonya has done a great deal of academic writing and has worked in the publishing sector as an indexer, transcriber, editor and bookseller, but her real love is writing. In recent years she has taken a keen interest in popular culture, specifically holiday themes. Her previous work includes *Halloween Trivia* and *Christmas Carols: The Stories Behind the Songs*, both published by Blue Bike Books. Tonya is the mother of three daughers.